THE KIDS' STUFF™ BOOK OF
READING
AND
LANGUAGE ARTS
FOR
THE MIDDLE GRADES

by
Imogene Forte
Marjorie Frank
Joy MacKenzie

Cover by Susan Eaddy
Illustrated by Kathleen Bullock
Edited by Jennifer Goodman and Sally Sharpe

ISBN 0-86530-122-0

TABLE OF CONTENTS

Dear Teacher Of Middle Grade Students 9
How To Use This Book 10

VOCABULARY 11
The Case Of The Missing Prefixes (Prefixes) 12
Words That Trip Lightly On The Tongue (Word Appreciation) 13
Do The Suffix Shuffle (Suffixes) 14
Whose Roots? (Prefixes, Suffixes, Roots) 15
Which Box? (Word Classification) 16
Supremely Sophisticated Sayings (Word Expansion) 17
What's The Difference? (Word Discrimination) 18
Synonyms On A Shoestring (Synonyms) 19
Synonym Silhouettes (Synonyms) 20
Space Invaders (Synonyms) 22
Antonym Bingo (Antonyms) 24
Teakettle (Homonyms) 25
Keeping An Eye On Idioms (Idioms) 26
Some Pun Fun (Puns) 27
Would A Marmot Wear A Monocle? (New Words) 28
Parade Of Words (New Words) 29
What Would You Do With A Quadruped? (New Words) 30
Definitely Dilly Definitions (New Words) 31
Where Would You Find It? (New Words) 32
Vocabulary Pin-Ups (New Words) 33
Guess & Check (Context Clues) 34
Choose With Care (Connotation) 35
Double Trouble (Multiple Meanings) 36

GRAMMAR AND USAGE 37
Capital V.I.P. (Capitalization) 38
How's Your Capital Eye? (Punctuation/Capitalization) 39
Punctuation Power (Punctuation) 40
Popularity Poll (Punctuation) 42
Hinkey Pinkeys (Nouns & Adjectives) 43
"Common-Tater" (Common & Proper Nouns) 44
A Verbal Agreement (Subject-Verb Agreement) 45
Plurals Please! (Plural Nouns) 46
Plenty of Pronouns (Pronouns) 47
All About Pronouns (Pronouns) 48
In, On, Above, About & Beyond Prepositions (Prepositions) 49
What's The Object? (Direct & Indirect Objects) 50
Lots O' Links (Linking Verbs) 51
Contraction Action (Contractions) 52
More Contraction Action (Contractions) 53
Tell It Like It Is (Parts of Speech) 54
I Know My Parts Of Speech (Parts of Speech) 55
Your Chance To Sparkle (Parts of Speech) 56
Alarm Alert! (Parts of Speech) 57
Bumper Stickers (Sentences) 58
Six-Way Sentences (Sentences) 60
Phonetic Phunhouse (Phonetic Spelling) 61
Dispel The Demons (Spelling) 62

READING 63

Who Is Reading What? (Associations) 64
Misplaced Prose (Associations) 66
Diving for Analogies (Associations) 67
Comic Conclusions (Drawing Conclusions) 68
Category Shuffle (Classifying) 69
Negative Ned (Fact and Opinion) 70
Reporter's Roundup (Relevant and Irrelevant Info) 72
Do You Believe Everything You Read? (Fact and Opinion) 73
Lasting Effects (Cause and Effect) 74
All For A Good Cause (Cause and Effect) 75
Fact or Fiction? (Fact and Fiction) 76
In The Mood (Identifying Mood) 77
Character Wheel (Character Traits) 78
Reading Between The Lines (Inferences and Outcomes) 80
The Human Hoax (Author's Purpose) 82
The Topic Is Penguins (Main Idea) 83
Test Your Knowledge (Reading to Verify Answers) 84
Cereal Circus (Reading For A Specific Purpose) 85
Clues and Views From The Morning News (Reading to Answer Questions) 86
Magazine Mania (Reading to Answer Questions) 88
Hurricane In A Hurry (Reading to Find Details) 89
Who? What? When? Where? (Reading to Find Details) 90
Princess In Peril (Reading to Find Details) 91
A San Francisco Puzzler (Recalling Information) 92
No End In Sight (Predicting Outcomes) 94
More Than One Viewpoint (Point of View) 97
Personalities Personified (Plot and Sequence) 98
Story-Bored? Try Story Boards! (Plot and Sequence) 100
Create A Cartoon (Sequencing) 101
Out Of Order (Sequencing) 102
Western Onion Special (Summarizing) 103
The Other Side Of The Story (Value Judgements) 104
A Halloween Night Visitor (Visualization) 106
Not An Ordinary Morning (Visualization) 107
Oh, Mother! (Visualization) 108

WRITING 109

Words On Wheels (Word Choice) 110
Brown Bag Mysteries (Descriptions) 111
Now You See It, Now You Don't (Descriptions) 112
Don't Be Afraid Of Big Words! (Paragraphs) 113
Rhinoceros For Sale (Advertisements) 114
You're Being Followed (Characterization) 115
Game Of The Name (News Articles) 116
Newsworthy Fairy Tales (News Articles) 117
Strictly Private (Journal Writing) 118
Attention! Attention! (Announcements) 120
Tall, Tall Tales (Exaggeration) 121
Getting There From Here (Writing Directions) 122
I'm Convinced! (Advertisements) 124
It's Your Business (Business Letters) 125

From Bach To Rock (*Setting Mood*) 126
Sound Search (*Sensory Appeal*) 127
Simply Delicious (*Sensory Appeal*) 128
Behind The Mask (*Emotional Appeal*) 129
Cool As A Cucumber (*Similies*) 130
A Duck Is Like A Stomachache? (*Metaphors*) 131
It Figures! (*Figures of Speech*) 132
Mixed-Up Mother Goose (*Rhymes*) 134
A Diamond Of Opposites (*Diamante Poetry*) 135
Original Epitaphs (*Poetry-Epitaphs*) 136
Quite A Quizaine (*Poetry*) 138
Weathergrams (*Poetry*) 139
Let's Limerick (*Poetry-Limericks*) 140
Paint A Poem (*Poetry*) 142
Framed Favorites (*Collecting and Organizing Ideas*) 143
Tasty Words (*Collecting Ideas*) 144
It's That Simple (*Outlining*) 145
Easy As A-B-C (*Collecting and Organizing Ideas*) 146
Graffiti Mural (*Collecting and Organizing Ideas*) 147
Getting It All Together (*Organizing Ideas*) 148
Found Writing (*Organizing Ideas*) 150
Better Beginnings (*Editing*) 151
Quick Change & Rearrange (*Editing*) 152
Words That Make A Difference (*Editing*) 154

STUDY SKILLS 155

Give Me A "C"! (*Alphabetizing*) 156
Read It! Do It! Name It! (*Following Directions*) 157
Pair-A-Gon Of Information (*Reading for Details*) 158
One, Two, Tree! (*Outlining*) 159
Errand Efficiency Quotient (*Organizing*) 162
Stump The Panel (*Preparing for Testing*) 164
Have A Happy Graph (*Graphs*) 165
Chart Smart (*Charts*) 166
Webster's Worry (*Dictionary*) 168
Define It Or Fake It (*Dictionary*) 169
Find The Common Denominator (*Dictionary*) 170
Missing Links (*Encyclopedia*) 171
Headline Heroes (*Encyclopedia*) 172
Historic Moments Mystery (*Encyclopedia*) 173
Here's Johnny! (*Encyclopedia*) 174
Index In Depth (*Indexes*) 175
How Far Is Far East? (*Reference Materials*) 176
Travelers Abroad (*Reference Materials*) 178
How To Be A Hero (*Reference Materials*) 180
Best Bet (*Reference Materials*) 182
Travel Logic (*Reference Materials*) 183
Aptly Adverbial (*Thesaurus*) 184
All In The Family (*Thesaurus*) 185
A Novel Blueprint (*Making A Table of Contents*) 186
Table Able (*Table of Contents*) 187

Dating Service, Anyone? (*Calendar*) 188
Border Puzzle (*Maps*) 189
Travel, Inc. (*Maps*) 190
Mapmaker, Mapmaker, Make Me A Map (*Maps*) 192
Invitation To Ellefont (*Maps*) 194
Shape Of A Nation (*Maps*) 196
Global Scholars (*Globe*) 197
If Time Is So Short, Why Are Time Lines So Long? (*Time Line*) 198
Where It's Always Christmas (*Road Atlas/Zip Code Directory*) 200

TERRIFIC TEACHER TIMESAVERS 201
Vocabulary Skills Checklist 202
Grammar and Usage Skills Checklist 203
Reading Skills Checklist 204
Writing Skills Checklist 205
Editing Skills Checklist 206
Study Skills Checklist 207
A Good Way To Encourage Divergent Thinking 208
Parts Of Speech (*Activity*) 209
Parts Of Speech (*At-A-Glance Guide*) 210
Meet The Punctuation Power Force 211
How To Prepare A Report 212
How To Study For A Test 214
How To Take A Test 216
Idioms 217
Good Vocabulary Words To Learn 218
Prefixes/Suffixes/Roots 220
Meanings of Prefixes/Suffixes 221
Abbreviations 222
Homonyms 223
Antonyms 224
Glossary of Writing Terms 225
Try Writing These 228
Plan For Individualized Reading 230
Individual Reading Conference Check Sheet 231
Ring-Around-Reading Record 232
My Reading Log 233
My Plan For A Reading Project 234
Great Ways To Share A Book 235
Creative Out-Of-School Activities 237
Other KIDS' STUFF Books For Middle Grades Language Arts And Reading 239

ANSWER KEY 240

DEAR TEACHER OF MIDDLE GRADE STUDENTS,

Middle grade students are a special group indeed--part grown-up, part little kid. Their needs are unique, too. Nobody knows this better than you. Although they are ready for plenty of independent pursuits and challenges to stretch their thinking abilities, they still need the structure and sequence of a basic skills program.

This means that you have the busy tasks of providing activities that encourage solid, skill-based progress and of pushing the students towards self-reliance and independent study skills.

THE KIDS' STUFF™ BOOK OF READING AND LANGUAGE ARTS FOR THE MIDDLE GRADES was created with you and your middle grade students in mind. It contains a rich variety of experiences, both teacher-directed lessons and independent student activities--each built around an important skill in the language arts curriculum. The challenging and exciting activities have the sparkle and high-interest appeal needed to capture the attention of middle grade students.

We have purposely prepared activities that demand very little preparation for the teacher. We have also included lots of attractive pages which are ready to duplicate for students. In addition, you'll find a number of 5-minute activities that can be done in those extra minutes that "pop up" often during the day. You'll love the TERRIFIC TEACHER TIMESAVERS section, added to put at your finger tips almost 40 pages of the kinds of lists, resources and extra-great ideas you need in a hurry.

We have packed this book full to give you creative material to supplement not only your reading program, but your grammar and usage and vocabulary building programs as well. The STUDY SKILLS chapter gives you 45 pages of concrete, student-ready tasks to sharpen a variety of those important skills. Likewise, the WRITING section contains a hearty collection of experiences that will get your writers "growing" right away. Besides your basic texts, we think you'll find this your most-used reference for teaching language arts!

HOW TO USE THIS BOOK

This book contains five chapters covering the most important areas in the language arts: VOCABULARY, GRAMMAR AND USAGE, READING, WRITING, and STUDY SKILLS. Within these chapters you will find four different kinds of pages, each labeled clearly. They are:

Teacher Pages -- labeled with:

Each *teacher page* contains a complete plan for a lesson, designed to be directed by the teacher.

Student Pages* -- labeled with:

The *student pages* are ready to duplicate and hand to an individual student, a group, or the entire class. These are pages that students can do independently.

Project Pages* -- labeled with:

A *project page* contains an activity that will take more than one class period. It outlines a learning task that needs several sessions, or one that students can work on over a longer period of time.

5-Minute Fillers* -- labeled with:

5-Minute fillers are just that--learning experiences that can be done in just a few minutes.

These chapters are followed by the TERRIFIC TEACHER TIMESAVERS* section. It's all yours--to use as best fits your needs. It was designed to save you time, but you'll notice that many of the forms, checklists, and resource lists are student-ready.

There are a variety of ways to put these handy timesavers to work for you. For instance, the forms that pertain to reading might be put into individualized "reading" folders for your students. The SKILLS CHECKLISTS can be used for parent conferences or for student review. The OUT-OF-SCHOOL ACTIVITIES make fine homework assignments, or may be optional activities for kids to pursue on their own. Review this section often. You'll see just how many uses it has!

*You have permission to reproduce pages with these labels in quantities needed for your class.

THE CASE OF THE MISSING PREFIXES

Help the detective find the missing briefcases. Only one prefix fits with all the clue words in each set.

Prefixes				
DE				
PRE				
BI				
NON				
IN				
MIS				
TRANS				
UN				
DIS				
RE				
SUPER				
SUB				
INTER				

frost	port	form	light
mission	act	state	view
plant	port	atlantic	form
sense	stop	athletic	fiction
connect	please	appear	satisfy
annual	cycle	lateral	weekly
visible	active	numerable	sensitive
official	do	sinkable	kind
behave	take	spell	understand
pay	season	test	school
mind	write	tell	play
zero	divide	way	title
star	bowl	man	market

WORDS THAT TRIP LIGHTLY ON THE TONGUE

PREPARATION:
- Have ready a collection of words that sound "delicious" when spoken. (See the examples shown here.) Include your own favorites.

USE:
1. Read some of your favorite sounding words to the students.
2. Ask them to repeat the words quietly to themselves, paying attention to how the words "feel" in their mouths.
3. Talk about the sounds of different words and how words give different feelings and set different moods.
4. Ask students to suggest more words with wonderful sounds. Start collecting these words in a group booklet or in individual collections of "favorite" words.

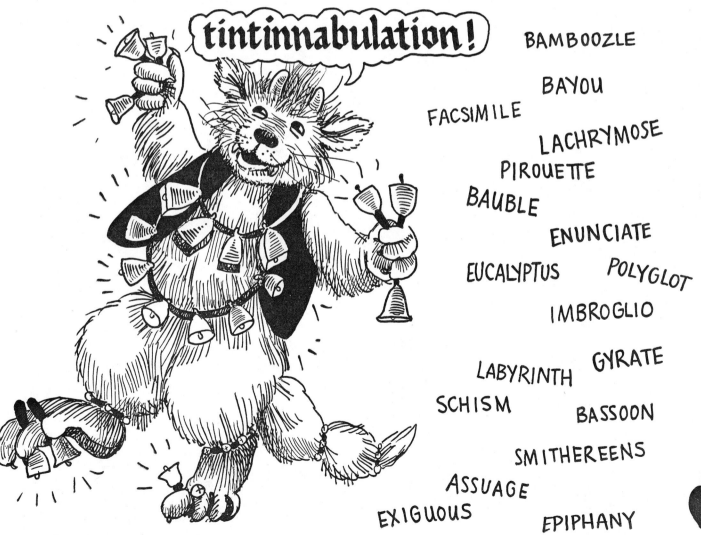

tintinnabulation!

BAMBOOZLE
BAYOU
FACSIMILE
LACHRYMOSE
PIROUETTE
BAUBLE
ENUNCIATE
EUCALYPTUS   POLYGLOT
IMBROGLIO
LABYRINTH   GYRATE
SCHISM
BASSOON
SMITHEREENS
ASSUAGE
EXIGUOUS   EPIPHANY

13

DO THE SUFFIX SHUFFLE

PREPARATION:
- Have ready plenty of 3 x 5 inch index cards and a copy of the PREFIXES AND SUFFIXES LIST for each student. (See page 221.)

USE:
1. Ask students to use the lists to make up "problems" such as these:

$$
\begin{aligned}
\text{silk} + &\underline{\hspace{2cm}} = \text{made of silk} \\
\text{mail} + &\underline{\hspace{2cm}} = \text{able to be mailed} \\
\text{tooth} + &\underline{\hspace{2cm}} = \text{without teeth} \\
\text{patient} + &\underline{\hspace{2cm}} = \text{with patience} \\
\text{friend} + &\underline{\hspace{2cm}} = \text{state of being friends}
\end{aligned}
$$

2. Have them write at least three, each on an index card.
3. Collect the cards in a deck. Students may reinforce the use of suffixes by drawing 10 cards from the deck and "solving" the problems. Students can work individually or play the game in pairs.

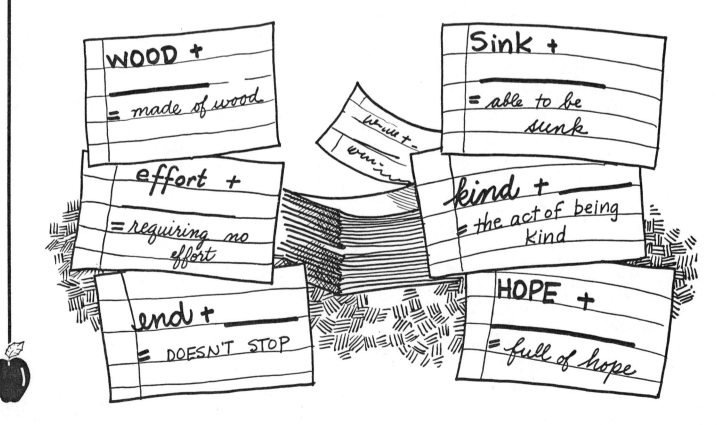

14

WHOSE ROOTS?

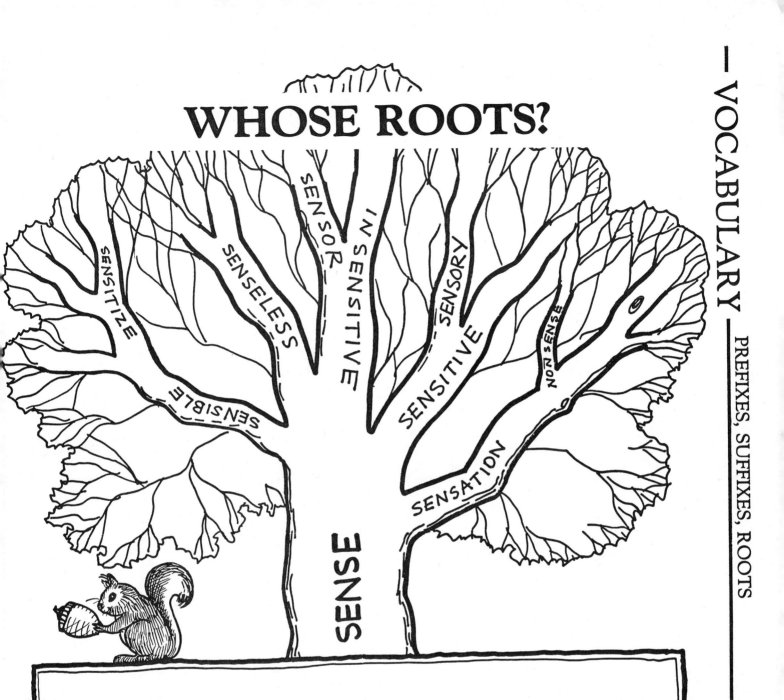

PREPARATION:
- Make enough copies of the PREFIXES/SUFFIXES LIST (page 221) for each student.
- Gather large pieces of construction paper or butcher paper, glue, scissors and markers.

USE:
1. Have each student design and cut out a tree with a substantial trunk and several branches. (Encourage individuality in tree designs.)
2. Give each student a copy of the **Prefixes/Suffixes** page.
3. On the tree trunk, have the student write any root word.
4. New words are then formed by adding suffixes and/or prefixes to the root on the tree branches. Students may add to the trees another day as they think of more new words that can be made.

WHICH BOX?

Each of the words below has something in common with several others in the lists.

Look at them carefully. Use a dictionary to find the meaning of any you don't know.

Then, classify them. That means--put together in a box all the words which fit together for some reason.

Give each box a label. The first one is done for you.

oboe	mechanic	risk	racket
addend	broil	knead	fraction
piccolo	teller	peril	mallet
surgeon	bagpipes	hazard	coronet
braise	saute'	warden	entymologist
polygon	helmet	marinate	harpsicord
puck	bat	centimeter	circumference
danger	jeopardy		

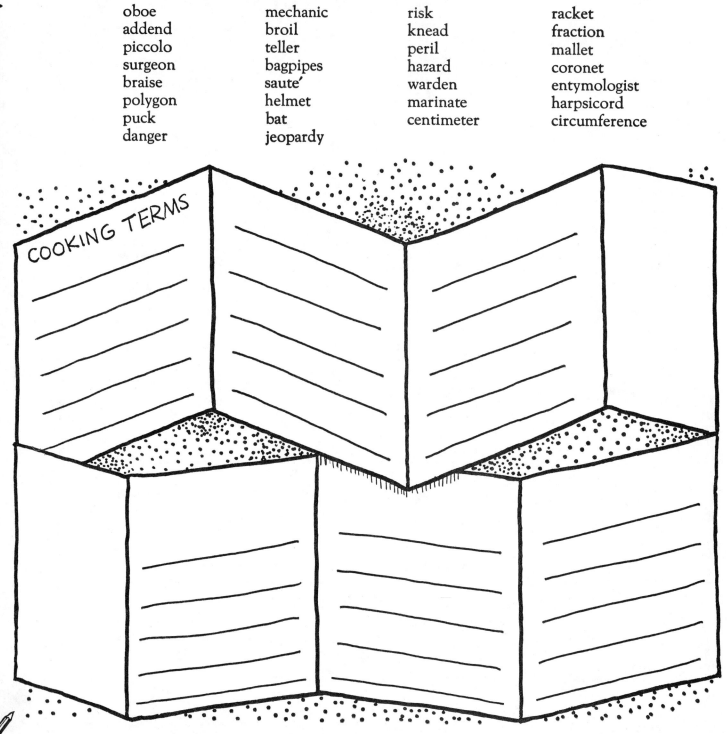

COOKING TERMS

SUPREMELY SOPHISTICATED SAYINGS

PREPARATION:
- Have available for students a list of common sayings (see examples below), dictionaries, thesauruses and copies of the following statement:
  A comprehensive existence of total arduousness in conjunction with the abnegation of leisurely trifling induces the juvenile male, Jackson, in the direction of hebetude.

USE:
1. Give students a copy of the above statement, which is a fancy way of writing a common saying. Together, figure out what its "plain" language version would be. (All work and no play makes Jack a dull boy.)
2. Together, take a few other common sayings and put them into sophisticated language.
3. Build a list of sayings to work with, then let students work in small groups or pairs to write their own sophisticated sayings.
4. Provide time for sharing, trading, and "translating" when the students are finished writing.

One rotten apple spoils the whole barrel.

Easy come, easy go.

Don't change horses in the middle of the stream.

You can't tell a book by its cover.

Easier said than done.

A dog is a man's best friend.

Don't count your chickens before they hatch.

Where's the beef?

He who hesitates is lost.

Never look a gift horse in the mouth.

A bird in the hand is worth two in the bush.

Put something away for a rainy day.

Time waits for no man.

WHAT'S THE DIFFERENCE?

Sometimes words look or sound very much like other words and are easy to get mixed up. Below are some of these words. For each group, match the correct word with its meaning by placing the letter of the right definition next to each word. Use your dictionary for help. Practice pronouncing each word.

_____ thorough	a.	a feeding bin for animals
_____ trough	b.	to adjust or modify
_____ through	c.	to abandon
_____ affect	d.	carried out to completion
_____ effect	e.	process of climbing down
_____ decent	f.	a song of melody
_____ descant	g.	to influence
_____ descent	h.	a tropical hurricane
_____ adept	i.	proper and fitting
_____ adopt	j.	stooped, drooping posture
_____ desert	k.	to discard or treat as unimportant
_____ dessert	l.	very skilled
_____ slouch	m.	food served at end of a meal
_____ slough	n.	in at one point, out at another
_____ tycoon	o.	businessman with wealth and power
_____ typhoon	p.	a result

Now, use one of the above words to fill in each blank below. Be careful not to get mixed up!

Do you usually do a _____ job of cleaning your room?
"Put on some _____ clothes," my mother is always saying.
My older brother has had quite an _____ on my ideas.
Marcia is very _____ at riding a skateboard.
I was so tired I decided to _____ off my homework.

SYNONYMS ON A SHOESTRING

Make this STRING-A-SYNONYM game for your classmates. Here's how!

WHAT YOU NEED:
- 3 x 5 inch index cards cut in half
- a hole punch and scissors
- about 10 shoestrings or pieces of yarn
- a shoe box or other box of similar size
- a dictionary and/or thesaurus
- construction paper and markers

WHAT TO DO:

anxious	bewildered	hostile
precise	naughty	scold
delight	obnoxious	jump
frightened		

1. Print each of the words given above on a card. Then, punch a hole in the corner of each card. Tie a knot in one string and thread it through the hole. Then tie another knot on top of the card to hold it securely into place. Tie strings to all of the cards.
2. On other cards, write three or more synonyms for each of the words above (one word to a card), and punch holes in all of the cards.
3. Put all of the strings and extra synonyms in a box. Try stringing each loose synonym card on the string of the proper word card.
4. Use construction paper to make a sign explaining the directions of the game. Paste this inside the box lid. Then decorate the outside of the box with the name of the game. (You can name the game anything you'd like.)
5. Find somebody to play the game with you. Keep a dictionary handy! Take turns timing each other to see who can string the synonyms faster.

SYNONYM SILHOUETTES

WHAT OBJECTS ARE HIDING IN THE PUZZLE?

Have your teacher give you a copy of the puzzle on the following page. The puzzle contains black silhouettes of several objects. All you have to do is color the puzzle following the code below. And, of course, you'll need to use the dictionary to find synonyms for words you don't know!

READY TO START?

Get busy coloring. The numbers after each line tell you how many synonyms there are for that word.

All synonyms of **bedevil**	Color **black**	(4)
All synonyms of **dowdy**	Color **bright yellow**	(1)
All synonyms of **impetuous**	Color **red or hot pink**	(2)
All synonyms of **intrigue**	Color **black**	(2)
All synonyms of **fundamental**	Color **orange**	(5)
All synonyms of **mucilage**	Color **black**	(3)
All synonyms of **glisten**	Color **bright yellow**	(3)
All synonyms of **design**	Color **bright green**	(1)
All synonyms of **chuckle**	Color **black**	(2)
All synonyms of **rectify**	Color **red or hot pink**	(3)
All synonyms of **fudge**	Color **bright blue**	(2)
All synonyms of **equivocal**	Color **black**	(5)

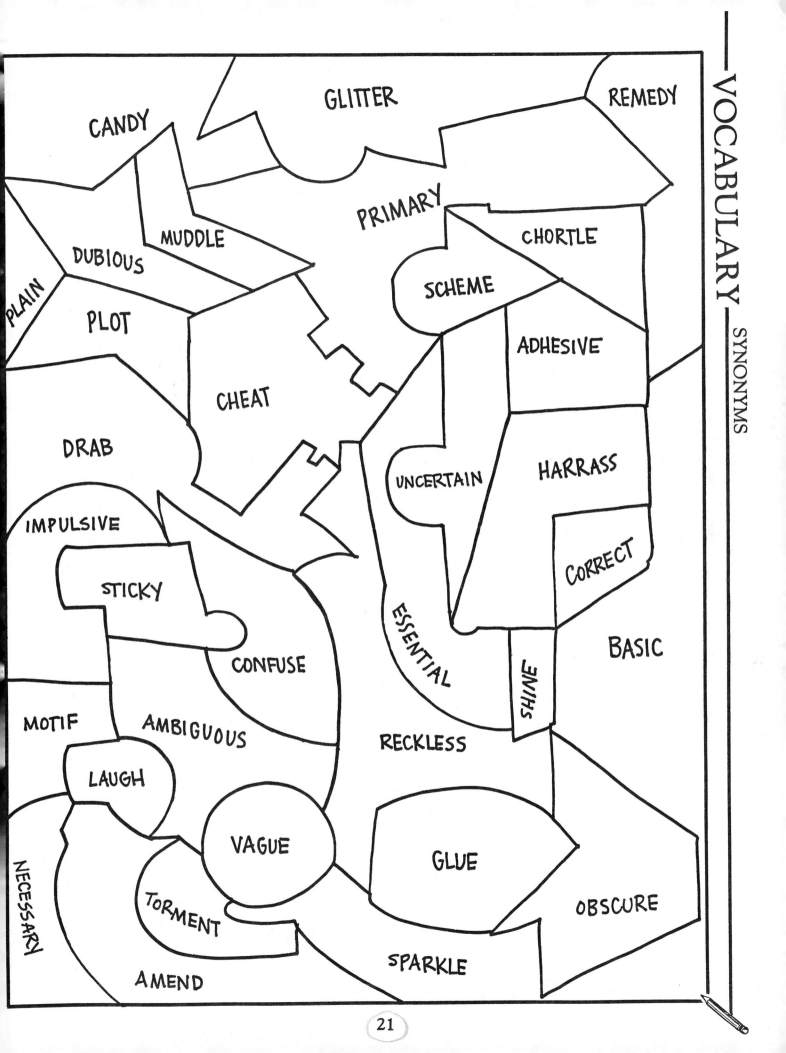

CANDY
GLITTER
REMEDY
MUDDLE
PRIMARY
CHORTLE
DUBIOUS
SCHEME
PLAIN
ADHESIVE
PLOT
CHEAT
DRAB
UNCERTAIN
HARRASS
IMPULSIVE
CORRECT
STICKY
BASIC
ESSENTIAL
CONFUSE
SHINE
MOTIF
AMBIGUOUS
RECKLESS
LAUGH
VAGUE
GLUE
NECESSARY
TORMENT
OBSCURE
AMEND
SPARKLE

SPACE INVADERS

Invaders from an unknown galaxy have infiltrated our planet! Can you find them and "blast them out"?

Look carefully at each formation. All the words have similar meanings--except for one. Find it and cross it out. You only have 15 minutes before it reaches your planet!

ANTONYM BINGO

Follow these directions to make a BINGO game of antonyms (opposites) that can be played by two, three, or four people.

WHAT YOU NEED:
- poster
- scissors
- markers
- lots of bottle caps, beans or pennies
- 3 x 5 inch index cards cut in half
- list of antonyms (Your teacher can find one on page 224 of this book.)

WHAT TO DO:
1. From poster board cut four squares (about eight to ten inches square). Divide each one into 16 spaces (four across and four down). Draw the lines clearly with a marker.
2. Look at the ANTONYM LIST. Write one of the words from each pair in a section on the BINGO CARDS. You can write the same word on more than one card.
3. Then, for each word you wrote on the BINGO CARDS, write its opposite on an index card. Shuffle the index cards and put them in a pile.
4. Now you are ready to play the game with two to three people. Here's how:
   - Choose a word from the pile of cards and read it aloud. Anyone having the **antonym** for that word on his or her BINGO CARD puts a bottle cap (or other marker) on that antonym.
   - Keep drawing cards until someone has all the spaces in a row (either up and down, across, or diagonally) filled with markers. That person must call out "BINGO" to win the game.

24

TEAKETTLE

PREPARATION:
- Ahead of time, have the students write pairs (or groups) of homonyms on small cards. Collect the cards in an old teakettle. (See HOMONYM LIST, page 223.)

USE:
1. A student draws a card and must use that set of homonyms in a spoken sentence. But instead of actually saying the homonyms, the student substitutes the word **teakettle**.

It doesn't make **teakettle** to spend 75 **teakettle** on a piece of bubble gum. (sense, cents)

2. Other students try to guess the correct homonyms. The student who guesses correctly gets to draw from the teakettle.

NOTE:
This game may be played by the entire class or by a small group--even by just two. And don't forget to add new homonyms to the teakettle as students think of them.

KEEPING AN EYE ON IDIOMS

An idiom is a particular language expression that means something different from what the exact words seem to mean.

For example, "keeping an eye on the baby" is an idiom. It does not mean to take an eye and lay it on the baby, as the words say. It means to watch the baby.

1. Ask your teacher to give you a copy of the IDIOM LIST from this book. (Page 217.) Add other idioms to the list, if you wish.
2. Choose one idiom you like.
3. Get a large piece of construction paper or poster board.
4. Find pictures to cut from magazines, or draw your own illustrations to show what the expression would mean if you took it literally (that is, if it meant exactly what the words say). Put the pictures on one half of the paper and write the idiom beneath them.
5. On the other half of the paper, draw or paste an illustration that shows what the idiom is generally understood to mean. Beneath this, paraphrase the idiom.
6. The examples on this page will help you get started. Try to finish your idiom project within a week.

RAINING CATS & DOGS!

BOY IS IT POURING!

PUTTING ON THE DOG.

WHAT A 'FLASHY' DRESSER!

DOWN IN THE DUMPS!

FEELING SAD

HE BLEW THE TEST.

HE GOT A BAD GRADE.

SOME PUN FUN

PREPARATION:

- Prepare a large "graffiti" mural for the wall by writing several puns on butcher paper with colorful markers.

USE:

1. Put the mural on the wall. Don't say anything about the mural until the students notice it and ask questions.
2. Talk about puns and then ask the students to add other puns to the mural.

I LOOK RATHER FINE IN A MONOCLE!

WOULD A MARMOT WEAR A MONOCLE?

For each of these, answer the question or follow the direction. Your dictionary will help you understand the meanings of the unfamiliar words.

Would a **marmot** wear a **monocle?** _____

Where does a **cowlick** reside? _____

Name three things that are **mucilaginous.** _____

Would you ask a **gammon** to dance? _____

Is it a good idea to climb into a **maw?** _____

Name someone who is **parsimonious.** _____

Would you find a **uvula** in an orchestra? _____

Could a **gargoyle** gargle? _____

How could a **vector** be harmful to a **rector?** _____

Could you keep ice cream in a **calabash?** _____

Describe a time when you were **obstreperous.** _____

Draw a picture of a waffle with a **wattle.** _____

Do you like your **physiognomy?** _____

Would an **obelisk** make a good pet? _____

Is a **charlatan** likely to be a **prevaricator?** _____

Name someone who is **fastidious.** _____

Would a boy's first violin lesson be **euphonious?** _____

Could a **lapidary** play leapfrog in a **lyceum?** _____

PARADE OF WORDS

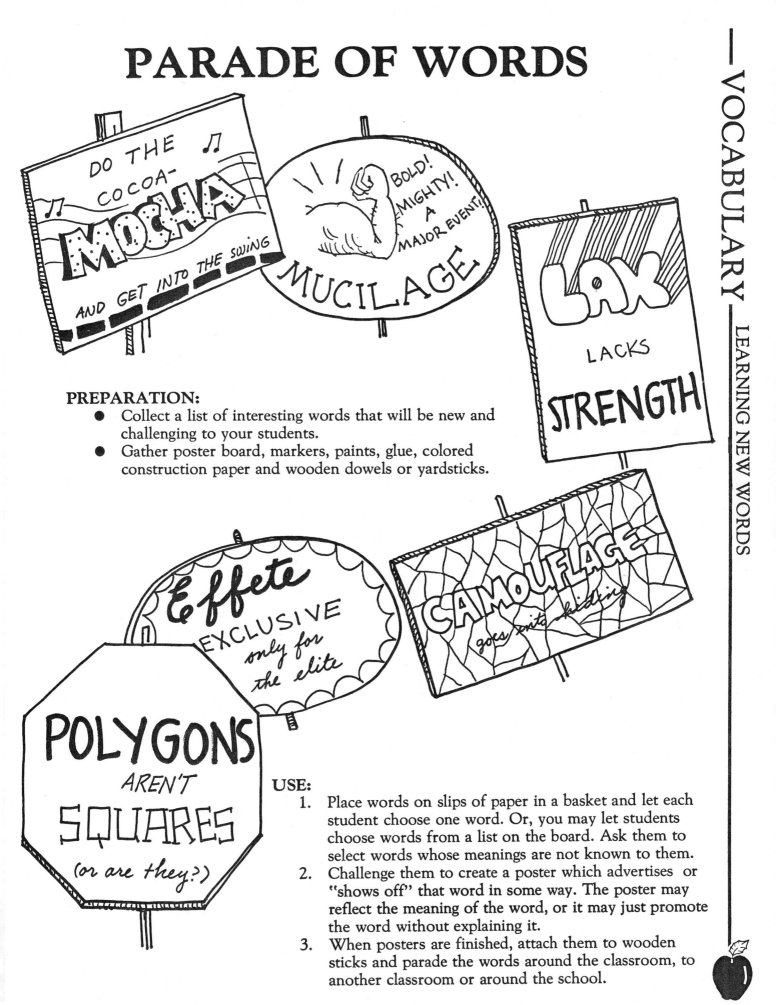

PREPARATION:

- Collect a list of interesting words that will be new and challenging to your students.
- Gather poster board, markers, paints, glue, colored construction paper and wooden dowels or yardsticks.

USE:

1. Place words on slips of paper in a basket and let each student choose one word. Or, you may let students choose words from a list on the board. Ask them to select words whose meanings are not known to them.
2. Challenge them to create a poster which advertises or "shows off" that word in some way. The poster may reflect the meaning of the word, or it may just promote the word without explaining it.
3. When posters are finished, attach them to wooden sticks and parade the words around the classroom, to another classroom or around the school.

WHAT WOULD YOU DO WITH A QUADRUPED?

MOOOO O O O O O

MOOOOO O O

FRAGILE: QUADRUPED

WHAT WOULD YOU DO WITH A . . .

Consult your dictionary, then underline the correct choice.

marquee	a. stand under it	b. salute it	c. plant it
projectile	a. throw it	b. eat it	c. dance on it
dirigible	a. ride in it	b. bake it	c. scold it
quadruped	a. deposit it	b. broil it	c. leash it
archive	a. research in it	b. chop it	c. feed it grass
missive	a. choke on it	b. mail it	c. rock it
decathlon	a. run in it	b. shampoo it	c. swat it
cadence	a. weigh it	b. pet it	c. dance to it
abode	a. extinguish it	b. clean it	c. scratch it
bairn	a. love it	b. paint it	c. file it
abscess	a. treat it	b. decorate it	c. shovel it
caldron	a. tickle it	b. swim in it	c. cook in it
aria	a. measure it	b. sing it	c. water it
edict	a. wear it	b. obey it	c. play it
refuge	a. hide in it	b. brush it	c. run from it
abutment	a. walk it	b. kiss it	c. fish from it
belch	a. gift-wrap it	b. stifle it	c. shake it
borough	a. move to it	b. sign it	c. ride it
labyrinth	a. get out of it	b. lick it	c. read to it
harrow	a. freeze it	b. bathe it	c. plow with it
enigma	a. yell at it	b. smell it	c. solve it
dromedary	a. launch it	b. feed it	c. pinch it
polyglot	a. talk to it	b. cage it	c. cross it out
chalice	a. laugh at it	b. remember it	c. polish it

DEFINITELY DILLY DEFINITIONS

Give your students a word that looks and sounds interesting, making sure it is one they do not know.

Ask each student to write a definition of the word.

— Janice —

mome: A rhyming mother rodent,

pruinose: having a nose like a prune.

silurid: a silver robot

verdant:

scapula:

macabre:

copacetic:

amok:

termagant :

jaborandi :

archive:

diadem :

Compare your definition with those of other students and with the actual dictionary definition.

Try to use the word correctly at least five times in the classroom during the next two days.

You may want to choose your own words — ones that you're sure are in your classroom dictionary.

WHERE WOULD YOU FIND IT?

Use your dictionary to help you learn what these words mean. Then tell where you might find each of them:

a lexicographer _____

an anvil _____

a primer _____

a villain _____

a caravan _____

an allegro _____

Answer each question 'yes' or 'no'. If you answer 'no', write where you would find the bold word.

Would you find a **pontoon** in a desert? _____

Would a **thesaurus** be at home in the ocean? _____

Might a **decapod** be found in a salad? _____

Could a **lynx** be found in a **menagerie**? _____

Might a **pedometer** be carried in a **caravan**? _____

Would a **thespian** be found in the refrigerator? _____

Might a **shrine** be found in a **pagoda**? _____

VOCABULARY
PIN-UPS

PREPARATION:

- Collect a list of vocabulary words which you would like students to learn.
- Gather magazines, construction paper, scissors, glue, markers, and crayons.

USE:

1. Give each student a new vocabulary word (or two or three, so they have a choice).
2. The student is to learn the meaning of the word and find or draw a picture which demonstrates the meaning. (Give them several days to do the searching.)
3. Have the students mount their pictures, label them with the vocabulary words, and share them with the class.

VARIATION:

Give each student a picture and tell the class that they have one week to learn (and bring to class) a new vocabulary word that "matches" the picture.

GUESS & CHECK

Read each sentence. The context (or use) of the underlined word should give you some clues to the word's meaning. Write down what you think the word means. Then write the dictionary definition and compare it to yours.

1. Both boys told convincing, though opposite, stories, and I couldn't **discern** the truth.

   _____   _____
   (Your guess)   (Dictionary definition)

2. Her bright yellow socks, neon orange dress, and purple frizzled hair made her look **bizarre.**

   _____   _____
   (Your guess)   (Dictionary definition)

3. Those **ominous** clouds make me think this isn't the day for our picnic.

   _____   _____
   (Your guess)   (Dictionary definition)

4. My friend Janice gave her **candid** opinion when she told me my new haircut looked unattractive.

   _____   _____
   (Your guess)   (Dictionary definition)

5. Maria has finished 18 who-done-it books this month. I've never seen such a **voracious** reader of mysteries.

   _____   _____
   (Your guess)   (Dictionary definition)

6. Judging from the number of falls Rob has taken today, I'd say he's a **novice** to skiing.

   _____   _____
   (Your guess)   (Dictionary definition)

7. The cashier **embezzled** $70,000 from the bank before he abruptly left town.

   _____   _____
   (Your guess)   (Dictionary definition)

CHOOSE WITH CARE

Words that are synonyms often have slight differences in meaning called connotations. For example, unusual and weird are synonyms, but weird has a more extreme or negative connotation.

For each sentence, consider the connotation of each synonym, then select the best one for that sentence.

The formal gardens behind the castle were _____
_____ .

cute   glamorous   fetching   elegant

The stray dog was so _____ , it looked as if it hadn't been fed for weeks.

slim   scrawny   slender

Our neighbors' _____ little boy is always playing harmless pranks on his friends.

loathsome   mischievous   wicked

We were _____ after being on the plane 28 hours with no sleep.

exhausted   weary   drooping

I _____ pizza, but I don't mind eating it once in a while if it's served to me.

abhor   detest   dislike

When the heavy brick dropped on his bare toe, the young child let out a _____ .

whimper   wail   whine

Some members of the audience _____ when the performer made a slight mistake.

howled   snickered   shrieked

Thank you for the snack. I hadn't eaten anything for a couple of hours, and I was feeling _____ .

hungry   famished   ravenous

DOUBLE TROUBLE

PREPARATION:
- Gather poster board, markers, magazines, glue and scissors.

USE:

1. Give students a list of words which have more than one use or meaning. For example:

rose	check	ball	light
ruler	trunk	scales	rock
sink	bark	star	brave
pitcher	slip	trip	fall
plate	hard	chest	racket
date	figure	drive	club

2. Ask them to choose one word and use magazine pictures or original drawings to illustrate as many meanings of the word as possible. The illustrations can be pasted or drawn on the poster board so that each student creates a DOUBLE TROUBLE poster.

CAPITAL V.I.P.

PREPARATION:
- Gather paper, pencils, and a timer.

USE:
1. Explain to the students that you are going to give them a limited amount of time to write a brief paragraph describing someone whom they consider to be a very important person. (10-15 minutes would seem appropriate for most groups.)
2. The object of the exercise is to write true statements about the person, properly using as many capital letters as possible.
3. Give the students a few moments to identify their people. When everyone is ready, start the "clock".
4. When time is up, ask each student to circle every capital letter and total the number.
5. Papers may be traded to check for proper use of capitals. If a capital is questionable, the sentence should be read aloud for the class to decide.

Note: It might be fun to do this activity several times with the goal of increasing the number of capitals as the time allowed decreases.

My Great Uncle Ed
by Tom Bull

Edward Fitzgerald Huckstable Cameron, better known to me as Uncle Ed, was a real character. Graduate of the great "University of Hard Knocks," as he loved to tell it, he eventually became the Ambassador to Bolivia in the days of the "Great Depression", and he was much ...

HOW'S YOUR CAPITAL EYE?

Below are examples of places where you see letters and numbers used every day. Use the copy provided to fill in the shapes, giving special attention to correct capitalization and punctuation.

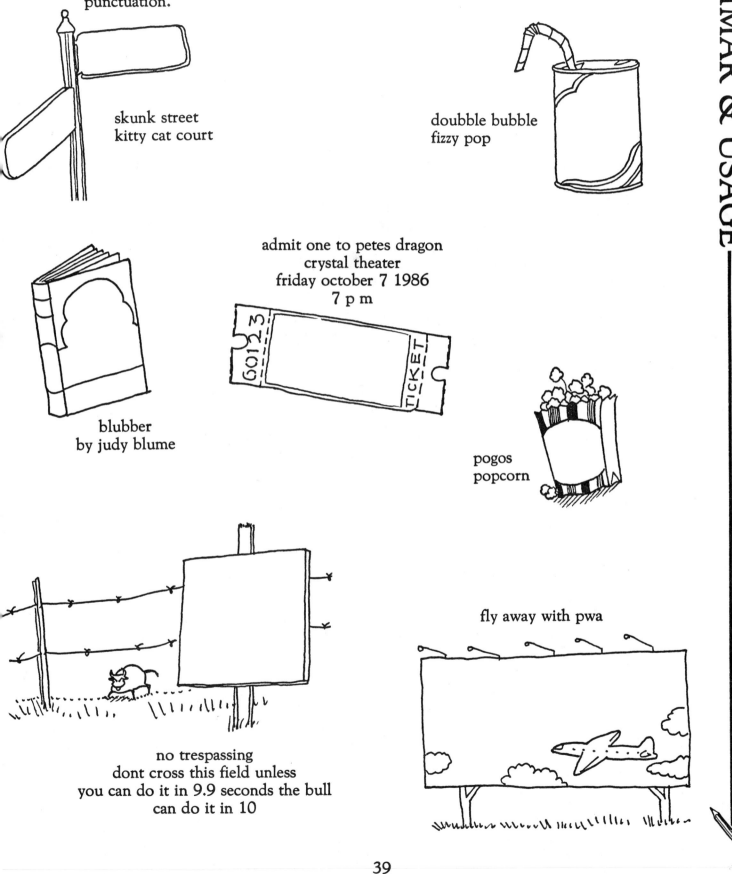

skunk street
kitty cat court

doubble bubble
fizzy pop

admit one to petes dragon
crystal theater
friday october 7 1986
7 p m

blubber
by judy blume

pogos
popcorn

fly away with pwa

no trespassing
dont cross this field unless
you can do it in 9.9 seconds the bull
can do it in 10

PUNCTUATION POWER

PREPARATION:
- Make a bulletin board according to the design on the opposite page.
- Supply the class with large pieces of poster board and thick markers or dark paint.

USE:
1. Use the bulletin board for teaching and reviewing the uses of the basic punctuation marks. (You may even give a copy of the page to each student.)
2. Ask each student to write sentences which use every punctuation mark example at least twice.
3. Let the students work in pairs to make large punctuation marks on pieces of poster board so that you have at least one of each. (More than one comma, period, apostrophe, and set of quotation marks will come in handy.)
4. Have the students write sentences on other pieces of poster board--one word per piece, leaving out all punctuation.
5. Have members of the class actually form sentences by holding individual words, while other members, holding the punctuation marks, position themselves properly to punctuate the sentences.

PUNCTUATION POWER

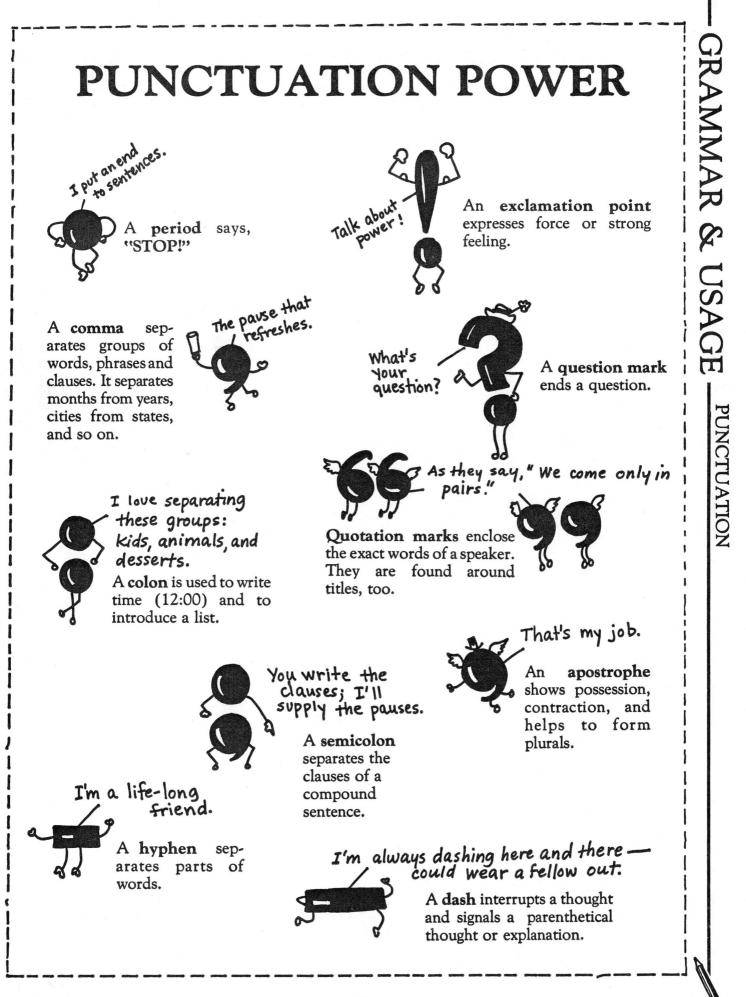

I put an end to sentences.

A **period** says, "STOP!"

Talk about power!

An **exclamation point** expresses force or strong feeling.

A **comma** separates groups of words, phrases and clauses. It separates months from years, cities from states, and so on.

The pause that refreshes.

What's your question?

A **question mark** ends a question.

I love separating these groups: kids, animals, and desserts.

A **colon** is used to write time (12:00) and to introduce a list.

As they say, "We come only in pairs."

Quotation marks enclose the exact words of a speaker. They are found around titles, too.

You write the clauses; I'll supply the pauses.

A **semicolon** separates the clauses of a compound sentence.

That's my job.

An **apostrophe** shows possession, contraction, and helps to form plurals.

I'm a life-long friend.

A **hyphen** separates parts of words.

I'm always dashing here and there — could wear a fellow out.

A **dash** interrupts a thought and signals a parenthetical thought or explanation.

POPULARITY POLL

Write a description of what you see in the picture. Try to use properly as many punctuation marks as possible. (You MUST use each mark below at least twice!) When you have finished your paragraph, count the number of times you have used each kind of mark and record the number below.

MY PROPERLY PUNCTUATED DESCRIPTION:

times used

. _____
? _____
, _____
" " _____
' ' _____
! _____
: _____
; _____

Which punctuation mark is most "popular" in your paragraph?

_____

Which mark came in second? _____

Which mark or marks are *least* "popular"?

_____

Do you think the results of this poll would describe the general "popularity" of these marks? Defend your answer.

_____

_____

HINKEY PINKEYS

Give the students clues such as those listed below. Tell them that the answer to each riddle is a pair of rhyming words. In each case the first word is an adjective and the second one is a noun.

Once they get the idea, middle grade students will love making up their own riddles to share with each other.

CLUES	ANSWERS
lemon gelatin	yellow Jello
a nervous burglar	shook crook
small wasp	wee bee
a sneaky boy	sly guy
an honest rabbit	fair hare
an overweight Chevrolet	Heavy Chevy
a disinterested Pinto	bored Ford
a fast hen	quick chick
sad footwear	blue shoe
a sneaky insect	sly fly
raining posies	flower shower
foolish William	silly Billy
a cooked newlywed	fried bride
a fat cement block	thick brick

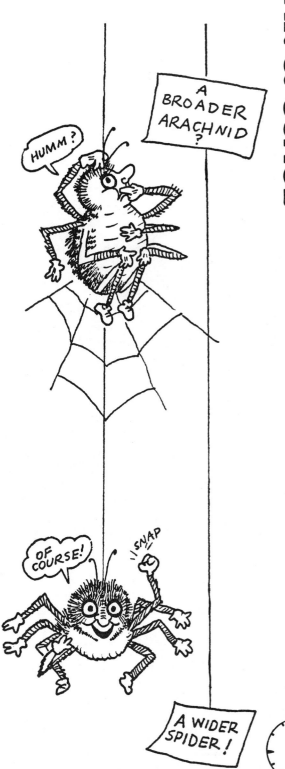

"COMMON-TATER"

SKY-SCRAPER
BRIDGE
RIVER
DOLL
TREE
CHURCH
BIRD
CITY
STREET
SHOP
MAN
BOOK
HORSE
MOVIE

COMMON NOUNS are merely the names of *non-specific persons, places or things*. This common-tater has a mind full of common nouns. List them in column **A**.

PROPER NOUNS are the names of *specific persons, places or things*. In the corresponding spaces in column **B**, see if you can create a proper noun for each of "Tater's" common nouns.

COLUMN A Common-Tater's Common Nouns	COLUMN B Coordinating Proper Nouns
movie	*Star Wars*

A VERBAL AGREEMENT

PREPARATION:
- Provide straight pins or tape.

USE:
1. Divide the class into four equal groups.
2. Ask each student in group 1 to write in large letters on a piece of paper a **single noun** or **pronoun** (subject).
3. Ask group 2 to write a **plural noun** or **pronoun** (subject).
4. Ask group 3 to write a **single verb.**
5. Ask group 4 to write a **plural verb.**
6. Ask all students to tape or pin their words on their chests so that the words may be read from left to right.
7. At the signal, each person must find a partner whose subject or verb agrees with his or hers.
8. When two students have formed a pair and are standing together so the subject and verb may be read left to right, the students should make up a silly sentence using their words.
9. Let each pair say their sentence aloud.
10. At the signal, the students should mix and match to form new pairs and new sentences.

PLURALS PLEASE !

PREPARATION:

- Make duplicate sets of flashcards using the following words:

life	shrimp	wife	scissors
lady	catch	penny	candy
sheep	ox	knife	pants
man	mouse	roof	chief
deer	tooth	library	fairy
family	fix	foot	piano
cliff	box	child	fish

USE:

1. Divide the class into two teams.
2. Set the two sets of flashcards (**not** arranged in the same order) on the chalk ledge several feet apart.
3. Explain that at the "go" signal the first member of each team will come forward, read the top card aloud, and quickly write the plural form of that word on the board above the word.
4. The student then looks at the teacher who signals "right" or "wrong". If the student is right, he or she removes the card from the set and touches the next teammate who goes to the board and does the second word. If the second team member is wrong, he or she touches the next teammate who tries to correct the mistake. (Teammates keep going to the board until the correct plural form is written.)
5. The team that finishes its set of cards first wins.

PLENTY OF PRONOUNS

Use the "ALL ABOUT PRONOUNS" guide (next page) to help you choose a pronoun for each blank in the story below. Then list, at the side by each coordinating number, the *kind* of pronoun you have chosen for each blank.

KINDS OF PRONOUNS

1. _____
2. _____
3. _____
4. _____
5. _____
6. _____
7. _____
8. _____
9. _____
10. _____
11. _____
12. _____
13. _____
14. _____
15. _____
16. _____
17. _____
18. _____
19. _____
20. _____

(1) _____ main objection to rock music is that (2) _____ is not what (3) _____ proclaims (4) _____ to be. When (5) _____ is first introduced to (6) _____ kind of music, (7) _____ might expect that (8) _____ should be gently rocked to sleep by (9) _____ . On the contrary, (10) _____ wild, raucous set of sounds is one (11) _____ might instead be better reserved for rocks -- stones, (12) _____ is, since (13) _____ music is likely to be able to jar (14) _____ from (15) _____ slumber. Perhaps (16) _____ is why (17) _____ is called "rock" music! Of course, (18) _____ would disagree! (19) _____ is (20) _____ prerogative.

ALL ABOUT PRONOUNS

(A Guide for Study and Usage)

A PRONOUN IS A WORD USED IN PLACE OF ONE OR MORE NOUNS.

PERSONAL PRONOUNS:

1st person: (the person speaking)	I, my, mine, me	we, our, ours, us
2nd person: (the person being spoken to)	you, your, yours	you, your, yours
3rd person:	he, his, him, she her, hers, it, its	they, their, theirs, them

REFLEXIVE PRONOUNS:
(self - selves form of personal pronouns)

myself	ourselves
yourself	yourselves
himself, herself, itself	themselves

(There is no such word as hisself or theirselves!)

RELATIVE PRONOUNS:
(used to begin adjective clauses)

who whose whom which that

INTERROGATIVE PRONOUNS:
(used in questions)

Who? Whose? Whom? Which? What?

DEMONSTRATIVE PRONOUNS:
(used to point out)

this that these those

INDEFINITE PRONOUNS:
(NOT referring to a *specific* person, place or thing)

all	both	few	nobody	some
another	each	many	none	somebody
any	either	more	no one	someone
anybody	everybody	most	one	
anyone	everyone	much	other	
anything	everything	neither	several	

POSSESSIVE PRONOUNS:
(possessive form of personal pronouns -- sometimes called adjectives or *pronominal adjectives*)

my your his her its their our

48

IN, ON, ABOVE, ABOUT AND BEYOND PREPOSITIONS

Write several prepositional phrases about this picture. Circle the preposition in each phrase. There are hundreds of possibilities. Here's a head start:

into the tunnel

above the tent

WHAT'S THE OBJECT?

Write two sentences for each picture. The first sentence should have a **direct object**. The second sentence should have both a **direct object** and an **indirect object**.

1. _____

_____

2. _____

_____

1. _____

_____

2. _____

_____

1. _____

_____

2. _____

_____

1. _____

_____

2. _____

_____

1. _____

_____

2. _____

_____

1. _____

_____

2. _____

_____

1. _____

_____

2. _____

_____

1. _____

_____

2. _____

_____

1. _____

_____

2. _____

_____

1. _____

_____

2. _____

_____

LOTS O' LINKS

PREPARATION:
- Each student must draw or cut from a magazine one large colored picture which represents a noun. (i.e. soup, man, animal, lamp, vegetable, etc.)
- The student must also write, in large letters on a 3 x 5 inch card, one adjective describing that noun.
- Masking tape and a large space on the chalkboard should be available.

USE:
1. Review the definition of a linking verb and ask the students to recall orally words that are frequently used as linking verbs.
2. Call on a student to tape his or her picture and adjective to the chalkboard with a sizable space between.
3. Then, in rapid succession, call five or six students to the board to write an appropriate "linking" verb between the noun and the adjective. Each student erases the word written before and reads his or her own new sentence. (The same verb may not be used twice for the same noun.)
4. Continue until all students have contributed a noun, adjective and several linking verbs.

CONTRACTION ACTION

Here are some handy rules for forming contractions.

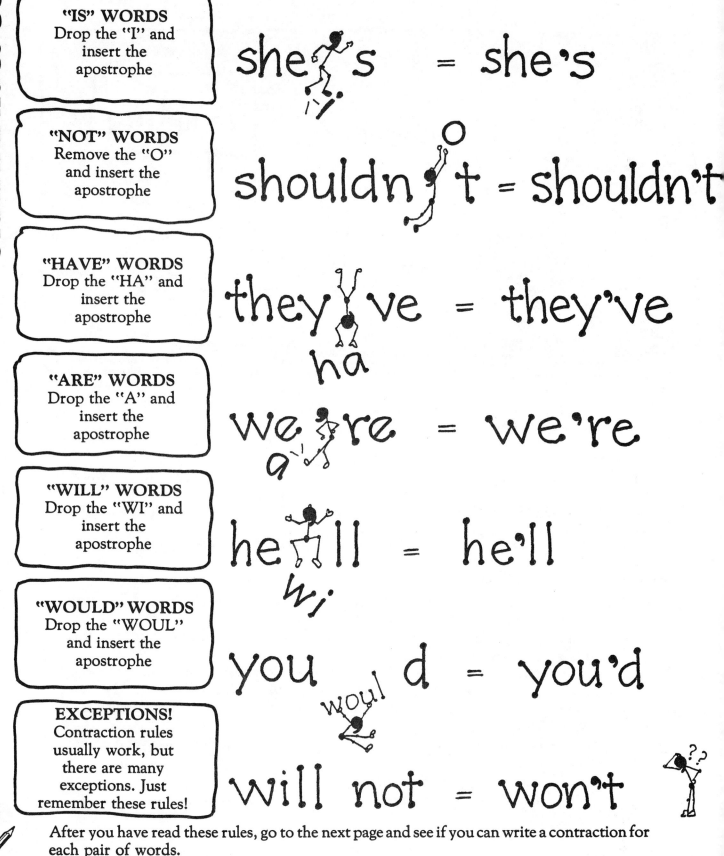

"IS" WORDS
Drop the "I" and insert the apostrophe

she's = she's

"NOT" WORDS
Remove the "O" and insert the apostrophe

shouldn't = shouldn't

"HAVE" WORDS
Drop the "HA" and insert the apostrophe

they've = they've

"ARE" WORDS
Drop the "A" and insert the apostrophe

we're = we're

"WILL" WORDS
Drop the "WI" and insert the apostrophe

he'll = he'll

"WOULD" WORDS
Drop the "WOUL" and insert the apostrophe

you'd = you'd

EXCEPTIONS!
Contraction rules usually work, but there are many exceptions. Just remember these rules!

will not = won't

After you have read these rules, go to the next page and see if you can write a contraction for each pair of words.

MORE CONTRACTION ACTION

Here are 45 pairs of words that make contractions. See if you can write a proper contraction for each one in just five minutes. That's about one every six seconds! Get someone to time you. Ready. . .set. . .GO!

they are	they would
are not	had not
could not	who is
you would	where is
does not	were not
she would	we will
she is	was not
that is	they will
you have	there is
you will	she will
would not	should not
must not	cannot
I have	did not
is not	do not
I will	has not
here is	he would
he will	he is
have not	I am
I would	let us
it is	what is
we would	who would
we are	will not

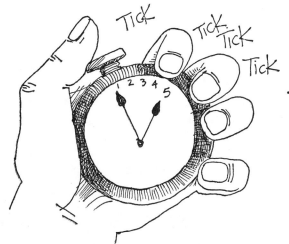

YOU'VE GOT FIVE!
CAN YOU DO IT?

TELL IT LIKE IT IS

Write a descriptive sentence for each picture, using the prescribed pattern. (You may use articles and conjunctions.)

1. _____ _____

Noun, subject   adjective phrase

_____ _____ _____ .

verb   adjective   direct object

2. _____ _____ _____ _____

noun   verb   direct obj.   prep. phrase

_____ .

3. _____ _____ _____ _____

adjective   noun   verb   indirect object

_____ _____ .

direct object   adverb

4. _____ _____ _____

adverb   noun   verb

_____ .

prepositional phrase

5. _____ _____ _____ _____

participle (adj.)   noun   verb   indirect obj.

_____ _____ .

direct object   adverbial phrase

Use the back of your paper to make some pictures and prescriptions of your own. See if your friends can do them!

I KNOW
MY PARTS OF SPEECH

PREPARATION:
- Gather poster board or tagboard, magazines, scissors, paste and string or fishing line.

USE:
1. Select four committees to draw and cut from poster board or tagboard the words *noun*, *verb*, *adjective*, and *adverb*. (Words should be about 1 1/2 feet high and written in cursive.) Hang them from the ceiling with fishing line or string, or, if necessary, place them on the bulletin board or wall.
2. Give each student an old magazine or two and ask him or her to cut out words that fit into the four classes.

3. Students may paste their nouns on the word *noun* after the choices have been approved by the "noun screeners" who check all "entries".
4. The same procedure is followed for all four parts of speech until the cardboard cutouts are filled.

55

YOUR CHANCE TO SPARKLE

Think of all the words and phrases you might use to describe yourself. Write as many as possible in the space below.

Now put yourself into the shape of a sparkling gem by creating a "diamond-shaped" poem about yourself. Use the formula below.

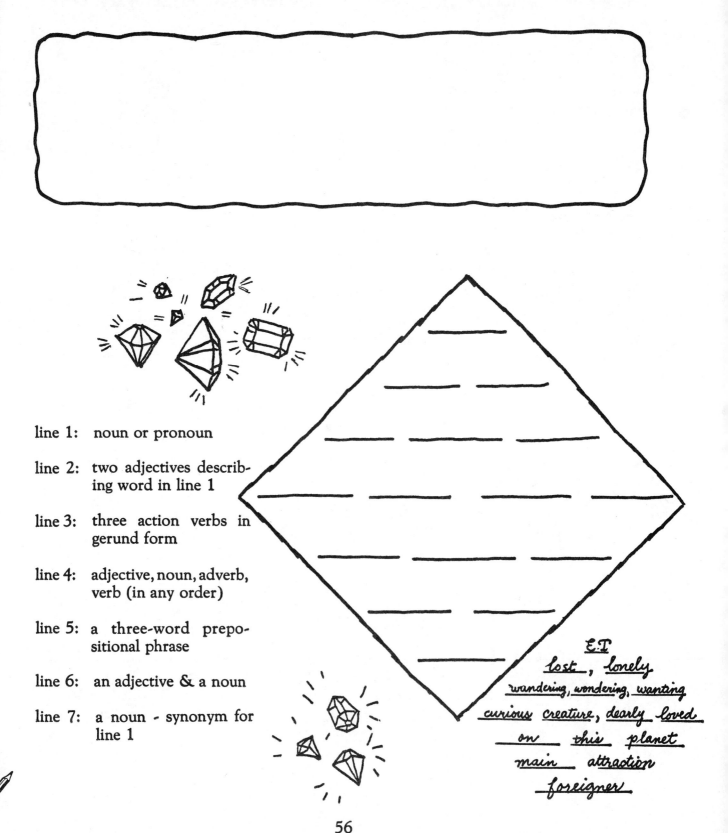

line 1: noun or pronoun

line 2: two adjectives describing word in line 1

line 3: three action verbs in gerund form

line 4: adjective, noun, adverb, verb (in any order)

line 5: a three-word prepositional phrase

line 6: an adjective & a noun

line 7: a noun - synonym for line 1

E.T
lost, lonely
wandering, wondering, wanting
curious creature, dearly loved
on this planet
main attraction
foreigner

ALARM ALERT!

PREPARATION:
- Locate an oven timer, an alarm clock, or a stop watch with an alarm.

USE:
1. Orally give the students a **noun**. (Choose one which has many possible modifiers such as *man, chair, part, story, day*, etc.)
2. Wind and set the alarm. Then have the students pass the alarm. As each student receives the alarm, he or she must give an adjective to describe the noun and then pass the alarm on quickly.
3. Students are *out* when the alarm goes off in their hands, when they cannot think of an appropriate answer, or when they repeat one already given.
4. Continue playing until there is a winner and then begin a new game.

VARIATION:
Give a verb; ask for adverbs.

BUMPER STICKERS

Some people put bumper stickers on the backs of their vehicles to share special messages. Others order special license plates that give clues to their names, hobbies, or businesses.

Try to make up a special bumper sticker for each character below. The catch is that each must be a complete sentence of not more than four words.

HORSE LOVER

HIPPO

SCULPTOR

FISHERMAN

MAGICIAN

HOT AIR BALLOONIST

HELICOPTER PILOT

MOTHER OF FIVE

NEWLYWEDS

Use the back of this paper to create some more of your own!

SIX-WAY SENTENCES

PREPARATION:
- You will need 5-6 pieces of chart-size paper & markers.
- Prepare a list of sentence fragments such as:

> scratching noises on the attic wall
> to warn the inhabitants
> having a forked tail and a long, jagged tooth
> dashed for cover
> awakened by a nagging conscience
> before his final leap

Standing there, so smug and tall, HAVING A FORKED TAIL AND A LONG, JAGGED TOOTH, he glared at us hungrily.

USE:
1. Divide the students into five or six equal groups.
2. Give each group a large sheet of chart paper and a marker.
3. Write six sentence fragments on the chalkboard.
4. Ask each group to collaborate to add to each fragment, creating an interesting sentence.
5. Each group's recorder should write the sentences on scrap paper as the group works and then should copy the sentences on chart paper.
6. Hang the completed charts, side by side, across the front of the room and read the sentences aloud to demonstrate the many possibilities for completing each of the sentences. Critique the charts for any errors and ask for corrections.
7. You might let the class vote on which group of sentences is the most interesting!

PHONETIC PHUNHOUSE

To do this page you will need crayons or colored markers.

Phonetic spelling sometimes looks like a foreign language. See if you can decipher the phonetic "language" used in these sentences and follow the directions to redecorate the house.

1. Kul'ər thə tü rüf pärts red.

2. Māk sum smōk cum'ing out uv thə chim'nē.

3. Ad prit'ē flou'ərs ə-lông thə wôk.

4. Māk blü kert'nz in thə ferst flôr win'dōz.

5. Kul'ər thə frunt dôr, gə räzh'dôr, and chim'nē broun.

6. Māk a smīl'ing fās in a therd stô rē win'dō.

7. Māk yēl'ō kert'nz in thə sek'end flôr win'doz.

8. Drô per'pl kert'nz in thə therd flôr win'doz.

9. Kul'ər thə dôr nob blak.

10. Drô a bī'sekl in thə drīv'wā.

11. Kul'ər thə hous grēn.

12. Ad en'ē thing els ūd līk to drô.

Write the phonetic spelling of your name here. (Your dictionary will help you.)

DISPEL THE DEMONS

PREPARATION:
- Prepare a list of words that are often misspelled or confused with other words.
- Gather large drawing paper, crayons, markers, colored paper scraps and old magazines for creating posters.

USE:
1. Display the list of spelling demons given below.
2. Ask each student to choose a word or pair of words and create a poster that uses mnemonics or some other "tricky" device to help students remember how to spell the chosen word(s).

   Note: Words may be chosen from the list, or a student may submit words especially troublesome to him or her.

3. Allow the students to explain their posters to the class. Display them for an appropriate period of time so that the students can become familiar with them.
4. Finally, ask one or more students to bind the posters in some manner to preserve them as a work-reference book to use in class, to share with other classes, or to place in the school library. A clever cover with a title such as "Dispel the Spelling Demons" will make the project more fun and will attract more users!

desert-dessert
whole-hole
loose-lose
who's-whose
principal-principle
shown-shone
quiet-quite
stationery-stationary
breaks-brakes
grate-great
occur
could
cough
every

their-they're
your-you're
weather-whether
threw-through
hour-our
through-though
friend
minute
women
tired
always
answer
success
neighbor

WHO IS READING WHAT?

On Monday afternoon, each of the following people checked out a book from the Readmore branch of the public library.

● Mrs. Makeover Mabry, whose hobby is re-doing old houses and making drapes for her friends.

● Justin Bestrong, the champion golfer, rowboat enthusiast, and member of the city's soccer team.

● Betsy Beontime, who conducts workshops on time management for young career women.

● Monty Moneybags, chief financial officer of the bank and the town's richest man.

● Tommy Tucker, who loves fishing, hiking and all things related to the outdoors.

These are the books that were checked out of the library. On the line under each book, write the name of the person who you think checked out the book.

Design a book cover for each of the readers below. Give each cover a title and an author's name.

1. Marcia Muchinlove, who is recently engaged and beginning to make wedding plans.
2. Bradley Boogiedown, a teenager starting his own rock band.
3. Jennifer Jellyknees, a 13 year old who is going on a two-week ski trip with some classmates, even though she has never been on skis in her life!

1.

2.

3.

Now describe a reader for these two books:

The Fine Art of FACE-MAKING

by Claudia Clownaround

HOW TO LOVE A PYTHON & OTHER SNAKES

STEPHEN HISS

SNOW WHITE... a weather almanac?

MISPLACED PROSE

Sometimes book titles are misleading. Here is a list of books bought under false assumption and laid aside by their owners to be found later in strange places.

Can you match the places with these book titles? Just for fun, add some of your own mismatches to the list!

Green Eggs & Ham
Black Beauty
Blubber
Big Red & Old Yeller
A Wrinkle In Time
Pippi Longstocking
Watership Down
Born Free
Superfudge
Trumpet Of The Swan

Dry Cleaners
Submarine
Hospital Accounting Office
Art Gallery
Dog Pound
High School Band Room
Whaling Ship
Lingerie Shop
Kitchen Recipe Box
Restaurant

DIVING FOR ANALOGIES

Dive into the treasure chest for words to complete the following analogies.

1. Hot fudge is to ice cream as hat is to _____ .
2. Basket is to eggs as sponge is to _____ .
3. Sun is to _____ as flashlight is to tent.
4. Sand is to shells as _____ is to rocks.
5. _____ is to boast as coat is to coast.
6. Governor is to _____ as president is to company.
7. Distress is to ecstasy as _____ is to wealth.
8. Phenomenon is to phenomena as person is to _____ .
9. Air tank is to diver as gills are to _____ .
10. Barnacles are to rocks as chicken pox are to _____ .
11. Band Aid is to cut as hug is to _____ .
12. Pride is to _____ as gaggle is to geese.
13. Insects are to entymologist as universe is to _____ .
14. Studying is to _____ as packing is to trip.

COMIC CONCLUSIONS

Finish the following picture sequences by drawing your own conclusions.

CATEGORY SHUFFLE

PREPARATION:
- Gather about 150 3 x 5 inch index cards and markers.

USE:
1. Give each student four cards. Have each choose a category (i.e.: tuberous vegetables, natural disasters, household appliances, diseases, Third World countries, equipment for games, desert plants, emotions, five-syllable words, etc.).
2. Have the students write the name of the category in the lower right hand corner of each card.
3. Then, ask them to write, in the center of each card, an item or word that fits into the category.
4. Put all the students' cards into a deck and shuffle well. The game is ready to be played by a small group.

THE GAME

- Deal each player seven cards. (Put the others in a stack, face down.)
- Take turns drawing from the stack. Draw one card at a time, and discard one card at the end of each turn.
- The first player to collect four of one category and three of a second category is the winner!

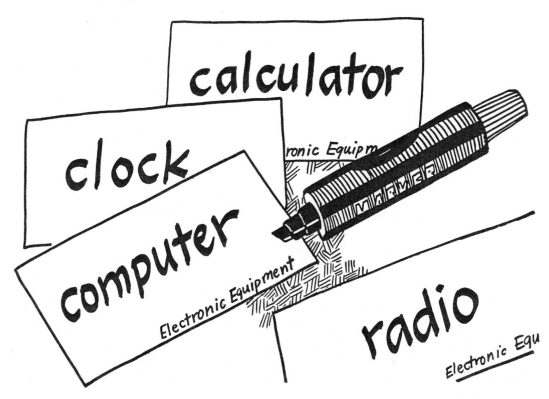

69

NEGATIVE NED

Have you ever noticed how two people look at an identical set of circumstances in two very different ways? Some people look at life in a positive manner, but others see only the negative side of things. Poor Ned falls into the latter category. He thinks about the worst that can possibly happen and expects things to get progressively worse. Because of this, Ned often gets his negative opinions confused with facts.

Read this account of a typical day in Ned's life.

"Time to get up!" called Ned's Mother. "The sun is shining and the birds are singing. It's seven-thirty. This is a great day to be alive."

"The sun may be shining now," whined Ned as he dragged himself out of bed, "but it is sure to rain soon. The weatherman predicted a 20% chance of showers today."

Ned was grouchy most mornings, but he was especially grouchy today. He really dreaded going to school. Now he was sorry that he had watched television last night instead of studying for his history test. He thought his teacher would probably be furious when she graded his paper. His mother tried to reassure him by telling him that she thought most teachers were kind and understanding.

"Not this teacher!" Ned retorted. "I can tell by the look in her eyes that she likes girls better than she likes boys."

"Ned," said his Mother, "it seems pretty unfair to come to that conclusion just from a look in someone's eyes."

Ned complained about everything he ate for breakfast. After breakfast, he left the sandwich that his mother had prepared for him on the kitchen counter. Without looking at the sandwich, Ned assumed that it was smoked turkey, his least favorite sandwich. He realized that he would have two choices at lunch—to go without food or to get something from the school vending machines. Because he was worrying about the problems of the day, Ned left his overdue library book on the counter next to the sandwich. Poor Ned! As a result of his negative outlook, he had another lousy day.

List six facts you found in Ned's story.

1. _____

2. _____

3. _____

4. _____

5. _____

6. _____

List six opinions from the story.

1. _____

2. _____

3. _____

4. _____

5. _____

6. _____

REPORTER'S ROUNDUP

Randy, the roving reporter, gathered all the facts plus some interesting tidbits for tomorrow's feature story. Now his task is to organize and summarize only the important facts for the report.

Help Randy write the story.

1.) Read the bulletin carefully.
2.) Underline the most important information.
3.) Draw a line through the unnecessary sentences or phrases.
4.) Summarize the special report in as few words as possible.

BULLETIN: At 2:00 on a beautiful Wednesday afternoon, July 6, 1985, Janis Jones had a terrible car accident. She ran into Mrs. Grouch's car, which was parked in front of Stone's Drugstore on the corner of Main and King. Janis suddenly had to put on her brakes so she wouldn't hit Freckles, the town dog. When she braked, she ran into Mrs. Grouch's car. Freckles has been around town for a long time, so everybody loves him and watches out for him. Fortunately, Mrs. Grouch was not in her car, but was eating lunch inside the drugstore. She always eats lunch at the drugstore. Janis, who has red hair and green eyes, works at Stone's Drugstore and is the best sales girl Mr. Stone has ever had. She was on her way to work when the accident occurred. Mr. Stone and Mrs. Grouch both rushed out of the store when they heard the noise. Mrs. Grouch, the meanest lady in town, was so mad that her hair was standing straight up and her face was beet red. She

stomped her foot and said that her red Cadillac would never be the same again. Then she started crying and ran inside. Janis, of course, tried to apologize and told Mrs. Grouch that she would pay for any damages. The police arrived soon after that and wrote a report. Then Mrs. Grouch's car was towed away and the police took her home. Freckles, meanwhile, was stretched out lazily under an elm tree across the street.

DO YOU BELIEVE EVERYTHING YOU READ?

PREPARATION:

- Cut large, colorful advertisements from magazines (at least seven or eight). Choose ads which are factual as well as those that suggest results or benefits that may not be true.
- Mount each ad on stiff construction paper or cardboard.

USE:

1. Show the class one advertisement, asking such questions as:

   - What does the ad say literally?
   - What does it want you to believe?
   - Is there a discrepancy between what it actually says and what it asks you to believe?
   - To what human need or emotion does the ad appeal?
   - Point out the specific words or parts of the ad which make the strongest appeal.
   - Is there an untrue statement? Is there a double meaning involved?

2. Repeat the procedure with several examples, discussing the differences between those based on fact and those based on opinion.

3. Ask students to look for ads (magazine or T.V.) and note the information that is factual as well as that which is opinion.

LASTING EFFECTS

PREPARATION:
- Supply each student with scissors, an envelope, a copy of the cause/effect strips (below), and a copy of the next page, "All For A Good Cause".

USE:
- Ask the students to cut the cause/effect strips (below) on all dotted lines, and to match each cause with an effect.
- Have them complete the "All For A Good Cause" sheet and trade envelopes with other students for more practice in identifying cause and effect.

The peace talks appear to be doomed to fail.	Hurricane Henrietta was approaching ahead of schedule with unprecedented force.
The guests were gone and the tree was beginning to droop.	Today's senior citizens are more affluent, healthy, and interested in challenging, new outdoor activities.
Concerned citizens raised more than $1,000 in 2½ days to help relocate the homeless.	The glitter, glamour, and festivities were over, but the good memories lingered on.
Hang gliding is becoming an increasingly popular sport among people 50 and over.	The countries' spokespersons simply would not listen to each other or try to see any viewpoint other than their own.
Houses had been boarded up, boats tied fast, and the whole beach area evacuated.	Once the fire was out of control, the residents of the tenement huddled together and watched their worldly possessions burn.

ALL FOR A GOOD CAUSE

Decide whether each statement describes a cause or an effect. If it is a cause, write an effect to go with it. If it is an effect, write a cause.

Then, cut on all dotted lines and put them in an envelope. See if a classmate can match the causes and effects correctly.

The music store had never had so many requests for one record in its 27 years of business.	
Brad ended up with a broken collar bone, two cracked ribs, a concussion, and several bad cuts.	
The 6th graders insisted they had seen a U.F.O. on the night of their desert camping trip.	
Susan spent six hours over the weekend practicing her gymnastics routine.	
Janice had 26 cents left in her bank account and she had already used three weeks' allowance.	
Hundreds of acres of forest land in the county had been cut down by the lumber companies in the last year.	

75

FACT OR FICTION?

PREPARATION:
- Print sentences and short paragraphs on index cards. Be sure to include an equal number of both fact and fiction selections. (Students may contribute these.)
- Place the selections in a box labeled SELECTIONS. Provide two additional boxes. Label one FACT and one FICTION.

USE:
Ask the students to:
1. Read the selections.
2. Decide whether each statement or paragraph is fact or fiction, and place it in the appropriate FACT or FICTION box.
3. After all cards have been placed in either the FACT or FICTION box, compare answers with another student.
4. Return all selections to the SELECTION box and add one sentence or paragraph.

IN THE MOOD

In these excerpts from "Cinderella" the storyteller has used key words and phrases to create a definite mood or feeling. Read the excerpts and identify the mood or feeling of each one by underlining the key words or phrases.

● *Poor, poor Cinderella. She was assigned the lowest, most menial chores in the household. Her wardrobe contained only outdated, tattered and torn castoffs from her stepsisters' closets. Even so, in her dark, dusty corner among the ashes and cinders, she maintained a patient forbearance toward life.*

● *All day long, the wicked stepsisters giggled, gossiped and lazed around the house. Their rude manners far outshadowed the fine dresses and splendid jewelry supplied to them by their greedy mother.*

● *The dashing young Prince was as gallant and gentle as he was handsome. His fine clothing was accentuated by shoes and other accessories of quality and good taste. It is a small wonder that he was the toast of the town and much sought after by young ladies from far and near.*

● *The wicked stepmother's treatment of Cinderella was ghastly and inexcusable.*

● *The generous fairy godmother arrived just in the nick of time to save Cinderella from a fate beyond description.*

77

CHARACTER WHEEL

1. Read a biography or fictional story, paying careful attention to the personality and actions of the main character.
2. When you have finished, list character traits of the main character.
3. Then, make your own character wheel using the wheel on the next page.

   ● Print the name of the character and the book's title and author in the center.
   ● Put a character trait in each spoke of the wheel.
   ● Include pictures, notes, or quotes to explain the character's actions, to tell more about a particular trait, or just to add interest.

CHARACTER WHEEL

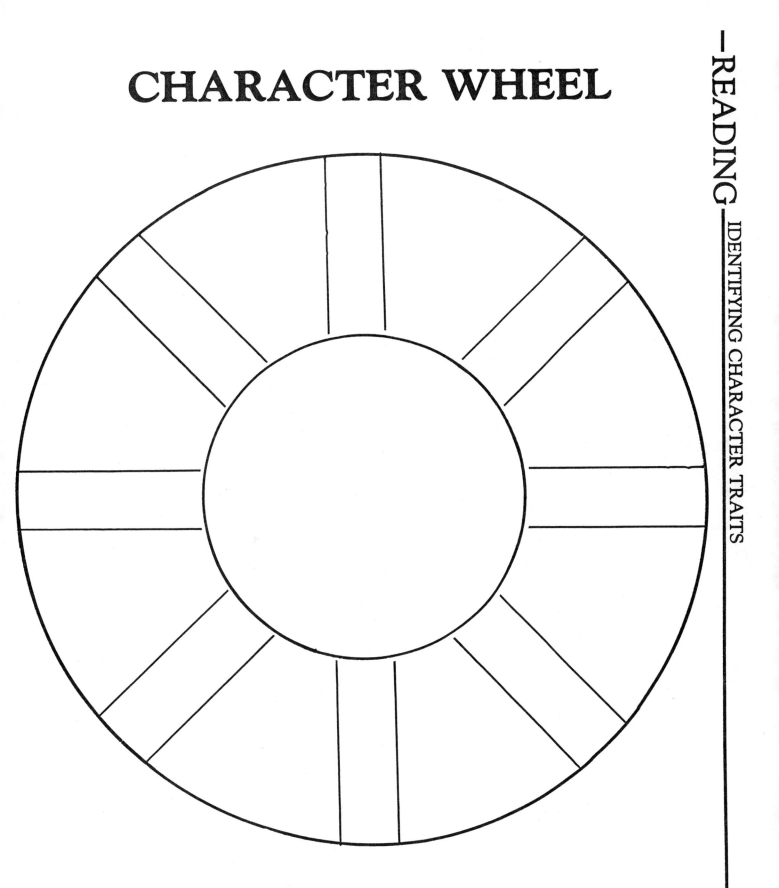

Note: Glue this on poster board for a sturdier wheel. You may punch a hole in it and hang it from a string.

READING BETWEEN THE LINES

Read the following story:

Even though her tentmates had conked out an hour ago, Julie was still having a hard time falling asleep. From all the rustling of sleeping bags she heard in the tent next to hers, it sounded as if the boys were restless, too. She'd never been afraid in the woods. It bothered her that she was so wide awake now.

Julie was restless partly because of the first night's excitement, but she was also uneasy about something. Those reports about mysterious happenings at campsites shouldn't have bothered her. They wouldn't have, except that the teachers who were supervising the camp out seemed upset when they first saw the condition of the campsite. The boys had overheard the teachers talking about the possibility of a connection between the reports and the terrible mess they had found. Maybe that's why the boys weren't asleep either.

"This is ridiculous," she said to herself. "If I don't get some sleep, I won't have any fun exploring tomorrow. If the teachers were that worried, they'd be up checking around." She crawled to the end of the tent and peeked out the flap. There was no sign of life. She snuggled down in her sleeping bag and finally felt her body beginning to relax.

That was when she heard it the first time--the loud crackling of branches and a heavy snort. "Did you hear that?" came a startled whisper in the next tent. The sounds came again, this time with a crash in the woods followed by a scream and scuffling noises just outside the tents. "Miss Matson!" a boy shouted. No one answered.

After a few minutes of silence, there was a loud panting and growling. By this time Julie had awakened her tentmates. They all huddled closely together. "Mrs. Bloom!" shouted the boys. "Miss Matson!" The teachers did not answer. It was quiet again.

"I'm going to take a look," whispered Julie. She was beginning to feel panicky. She crawled to look out of the tent. The boys were peering out of their tent, too. All of them gasped at the sight of the teachers' tent--torn to shreds with the contents strewn all over the campsite. That wasn't all. . .

READING BETWEEN THE LINES

What do you think the kids were doing in the woods in the first place? _____

_____

_____

What can you tell about the kind of person Julie is? _____

_____

_____

Does anything lead you to believe that Julie is an experienced camper? _____

_____

_____

What kind of "reports" might they have heard before the camp out? _____

_____

_____

_____

What do you think the condition of the campsite was when they arrived? _____

_____

_____

_____

Describe two possible reasons why the teachers might not have answered the kids' calls.

_____

_____

_____

Finish the story in a way that explains the "mysterious happenings" that night. Use the back of this paper.

THE HUMAN HOAX

The following paragraph was written to make you feel a certain way about wolves. Read it through once.

For ages, intelligent people have known about the ferociousness of the wolf. Years ago, pioneers and other folks told horrifying tales of vicious attacks upon livestock, chickens, hunters, and even children who wandered to the edge of the village at night. With its sharp fangs, ugly, yellow eyes, and swift, relentless tracking abilities, the wolf is a serious enemy to all of mankind. Few living creatures can outrun a wolf. Its teeth can tear apart a large animal in minutes. What's more, wolves often travel in packs--the most dangerous way of all to encounter a wolf. So, you had better beware any time you hear the bloodcurdling howl of the wolf. Remember what almost happened to Red Riding Hood!

What is this author's bias? What is the author trying to make you think of wolves? _____

_____

Now, go back through the story and underline any words or phrases that contribute to this feeling.

On the back of this paper, write your own paragraph with a particular bias. When you finish, trade papers with another student. Try to identify the biases in each other's writing. Point out the words and phrases that contribute to the bias.

THE TOPIC IS PENGUINS

1. Read the following article.
2. Underline the topic sentence in each of the three paragraphs.
3. When you finish this activity you are sure to know more about penguins!

Did you know that penguins living in the wild will never be found anywhere north of the equator? Most penguins that are observed by human beings are in zoos around the world. This is because not many people visit frozen lands where penguins breed and live. If you could visit Antarctica, you would find seven different kinds of penguins there.

Actually, penguins live a very dangerous life. Since they cannot fly, they are easy prey for other animals. They are equally in danger on both land and ice. Among their enemies are leopard seals, killer whales, gulls, and other large birds. The penguin tries to protect itself by flapping its wings, by swimming rapidly, and by leaping quickly from the water to blocks of ice.

Oil produced in a gland near the tail is used by the penguin to keep its feathers dry. A thin film of this oil is spread over the feathers by the penguin's bill and wing edges. This waterproofing is especially important since the penguin's small, stiff feathers overlap and grow very close together. Fluffy down feathers grow underneath to aid in keeping the penguin warm. It is this kind of natural phenomenon that reminds us of the marvels of nature.

This article is mainly about:
____ Antarctica, where penguins live
____ How penguins protect themselves
____ Penguins and other birds
____ How penguins keep warm
____ Penguin facts
____ Wild birds of cold regions
____ Enemies of wild birds

TEST YOUR KNOWLEDGE

TEST YOUR KNOW-LEDGE!

Information about each of these words or phrases can easily be found in the encyclopedia or other reference books. Without consulting any sources, write your best definition or explanation for each word or phrase. Then, check your answers with reference books to see how accurate they are!

1. Volcanoes: _____

_____

2. Comets: _____

_____

3. Neanderthal man: _____

_____

4. Photosynthesis: _____

_____

5. Gravity: _____

_____

6. The United Nations: _____

_____

7. Anthropology: _____

_____

CEREAL CIRCUS

PREPARATION:
- Collect several empty cereal boxes.
- Use the information on the boxes to create several questions such as these. Write each question on an index card.

  - Find three synonyms for tasty.
  - Which box tells where the Quaker company is located?
  - Write a story using only the words found on one box.
  - Tell which box presents its cereal most appealingly. Explain why.
  - Write a letter for a free offer found on one of the boxes.
  - List the ingredients from two boxes.
  - Write a letter to the manufacturer whose product seems to have the least healthy ingredients.
  - Make a list of all the compound words found on the boxes.
  - Create five math problems using numbers found on the boxes.

USE:
1. Place the index cards and several blank cards on the table with the cereal boxes.
2. Assign each student a specific number of questions to complete.
3. Require each student to add one question when she or he is finished answering the assigned questions.

CLUES & VIEWS FROM THE MORNING NEWS

Use a copy of today's newspaper to find answers for five of the following questions. Write the questions and answers on a separate sheet of paper.

1. What is today's biggest news story? _____

2. What could you buy on sale today in a downtown store? _____

3. What is today's weather forecast? _____

4. Name three movies you could see in a downtown movie theater (or theaters) tomorrow. _____

5. What was the leading sports story today? _____

6. Summarize one comic strip. _____

7. Find a house or apartment for rent near your school. Give the address and phone number. _____

8. Give the title and time of three T.V. programs you would like to see tonight. _____

9. Summarize the information from one front page article of interest to you. _____

10. Give the name and address of a store that advertises clothing you would like to buy. _____

11. Write all the information you can find about one person listed in the obituary column. _____

12. Describe something that has happened in a foreign country recently.

    _____

    _____

13. Summarize one editorial. _____

    _____

    _____

14. Find one item in the classified ads that you'd like to buy. Describe it. _____

    _____

    _____

15. Describe one cultural event advertised or included in today's news.

    _____

    _____

MAGAZINE MANIA

Select an article from a magazine of your choice.

1. Write the complete title. _____

2. Read the entire article carefully.

3. Write six key words from the article. _____
   _____

4. Write three key phrases from the article. _____
   _____
   _____
   _____

5. What is the article about? _____
   _____

6. What is the setting for the article? _____

7. Copy one sentence from your selection that gives the main idea or "punch line" of the article.
   _____

8. Do you think the article gives enough information? Why? _____
   _____
   _____

9. Do you think the headline or title really tells what the article is about, or is it misleading?
   _____
   _____

10. Write another headline or title for the article. _____
    _____

HURRICANE IN A HURRY

Read the paragraph below to find out about hurricanes. Then answer the questions below without rereading the information. Read the paragraph again to check your answers.

Hurricanes usually occur in the summer and autumn when the ocean is the warmest. The warm, moist air rises and then cools to form rain clouds. The rotation of the earth causes the clouds to spin like a giant whirlwind. Hurricane winds can blow at more than 200 miles an hour. The whirlwind sucks up the warm air in a spiral motion and then dumps the water on land in sheets of rain which cause floods. The eye of the storm is called the eye-wall. This is where the air spins the fastest. A storm surge is the most devastating part of a hurricane. It is a giant wave of ocean water that sweeps over a coast when a hurricane reaches land. The storm surge is like a giant bulldozer. It can change the shape of the land in minutes.

Circle the letter of the best answer.

1. The main idea of the story is:
   (A) rain
   (B) hurricanes
   (C) ocean waves

2. The eye of the storm is called the:
   (A) eye-wall
   (B) storm surge
   (C) whirlwind

3. The most devastating part of a hurricane is:
   (A) the storm surge
   (B) the eye-wall
   (C) the rain clouds

4. Hurricanes usually occur in the:
   (A) summer and spring
   (B) spring and autumn
   (C) summer and autumn

5. Hurricanes do damage on land by causing:
   (A) floods
   (B) blizzards
   (C) volcanoes

6. Hurricane winds can blow at more than 200 miles an hour.
   (A) true
   (B) false

7. Hurricanes occur when the ocean is:
   (A) warm
   (B) cold
   (C) quiet

Who? What? When? Where?

1. Cut a 9" square of construction paper.

2. Fold the paper into fourths, then open.

3. Fold each corner in so it touches the center.

4. On the outside of each flap write WHO? WHAT? WHERE? WHEN?

WHO? WHERE? WHAT? WHEN?

5. Write the title of a story and its author in the center of the opened square.

TOM SAWYER by MARK TWAIN

6. Write a brief description on the underside of each flap explaining WHO, WHAT, WHERE and WHEN.

Tom Sawyer by Mark Twain

7. Illustrations would be fun where you have room!

8. Make an interesting bulletin board display. Check out what the other kids have been reading.

PRINCESS IN PERIL

As you read the story of THE PRINCESS AND THE PEA, you'll be looking for specific details. For each sentence, underline the part that tells WHO with blue crayon or marker, WHAT with red, WHERE with green, WHEN with orange, and WHY with black. (Some sentences may not contain all of the details.)

What a Night!

1. Once, long ago, there was a prince who journeyed to far away lands in search of a true and beautiful princess.

2. But, alas, the prince came home brokenhearted because he could not find a young woman who truly *was* a princess.

3. One night, in the middle of a terrible storm, a knock was heard at the palace gate and the king went to see who was there.

4. There stood a young woman, drenched with water, who said that she was truly a princess.

5. To find out if the young woman really was a princess, the queen put one small pea underneath the 20 mattresses and 20 eiderdown quilts the princess was to sleep on.

6. When asked the next morning how she slept, the young woman answered, "I could hardly sleep at all because of something hard in my bed!"

7. Because she felt the pea through 20 mattresses and 20 eiderdown quilts, the royal family declared that she really was a true princess.

8. The Prince then married the young woman because he knew that at last he had found a true princess.

A San Francisco Puzzler

To solve the puzzle and find the hidden symbol, read the paragraph below. Then color the numbered spaces as directed.

San Francisco is perhaps the most beautiful city in the United States. May through October is the best time to plan a visit to this lovely bay side city. Sparkling blue water, a natural harbor, and steep hills give the city a unique charm. After visiting Fisherman's Wharf, one would surely want to take a ride on one of America's last operating trolley cars. For a panoramic view of the whole area, one may drive across the beautiful Golden Gate bridge. Continue driving through scenic Sausalito to Muir Woods National Monument.

If San Francisco is an ugly city, color the #3 spaces **black**.

If San Francisco is located on a bay, color the #1 spaces **purple**.

If the best time to visit San Francisco is winter, color the #7 spaces **orange**.

If San Fancisco has a Fisherman's Warf, color the #5 spaces **light blue**.

If you can travel by trolley in San Francisco, color the #2 spaces **lavender**.

If San Francisco has a man-made harbor, color the #8 spaces **green**.

If crossing the Golden Gate Bridge will give you a panoramic view of the area, color the #6 spaces **red**.

If there are no woods near San Francisco, color the #10 spaces **brown**.

If Sausalito is across the Golden Gate Bridge, color the #4 spaces **yellow**.

If San Francisco has steep hills, color the #9 spaces **pink**.

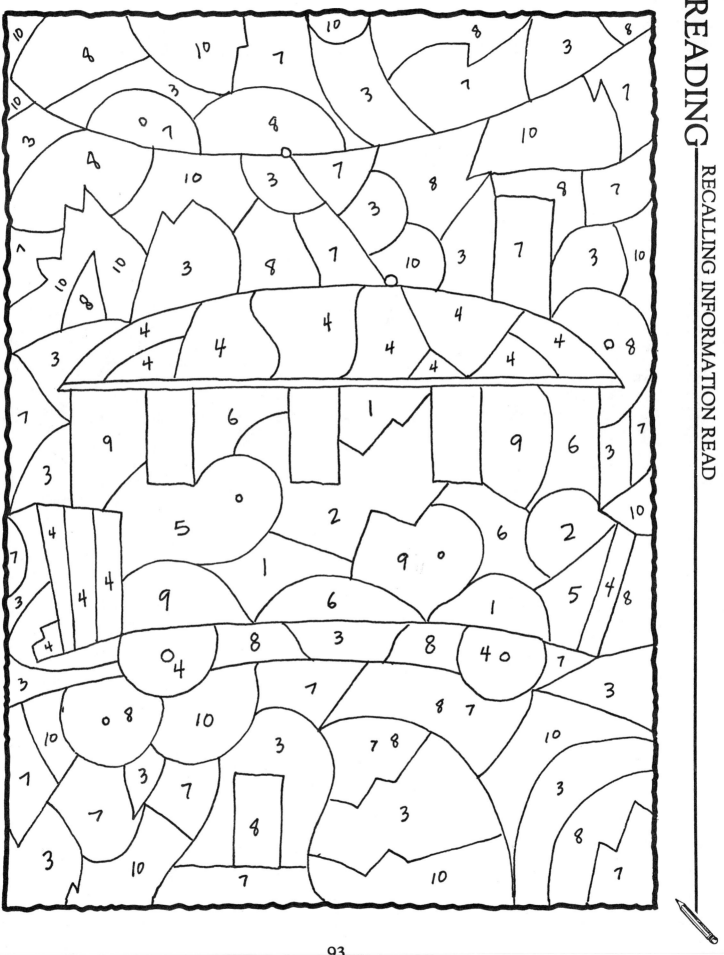

NO END IN SIGHT

Each of the story starters on the following pages presents a situation with several possible outcomes.

1. Try to think through each situation carefully to decide what will happen next.
2. Write your own ending for each story.
3. Add to the illustrations in the spaces provided.

Jennifer awoke in the middle of the night to the sound of the strangest, eeriest noise she had ever heard in her life. At one moment it seemed to be coming from outside her bedroom window and in the next instance from the bedroom ceiling. All the while a muffled rumbling continued to emerge from under her bed. As she bolted upright in the bed, too frightened to move, Jennifer tried to decide what to do. Should she make a dash for the door, call loudly to her parents, or hide under the covers until the noise stopped or someone came to help her?

Draw your own picture here.

_____

_____

_____

_____

_____

Kevin was all ready for his big trip. Traveling was his very favorite activity, and this was the day he had looked forward to for many months. Just as he was ready to pick up his bag to leave for the plane, the phone rang and all his plans were subject to change. A representative of the airline was calling to tell him the flight had been cancelled. He was told the airline would either reschedule the trip for one day next week, or give him two free tickets (one for himself and one for a companion) to use on any regularly scheduled flight within the next six months. Kevin was in a real dilemma.

Since school was starting next week, he wouldn't be able to take the trip without missing several days of school. He didn't want to cancel the trip, even though he would be able to get free tickets. He knew that his sister would like to make the same trip, but he had looked forward to going alone. Kevin's mother came into the room and said, "I know you will consider all the possibilities carefully in order to make the right decision."

_____

_____

_____

_____

_____

_____

_____

Draw your own picture here.↴

Wilma and Wiley had lived next door to each other all their lives. They were the same age and in the same grade at school. Most of the time they were good friends and enjoyed being together. Occasionally, however, they disagreed about what they wanted to do or how they would do it. Yesterday was one of those times.

On the way home from school, Wiley suggested using Wilma's ball to play "toss the ball". As they walked along, they passed the ball back and forth to each other. Wiley suddenly threw the ball very hard. It sailed right over Wilma's head. The sound of breaking glass told them that the ball had smashed through Mrs. Fussbudget's window. The door opened. Mrs. Fussbudget, the crossest lady in town, walked out and said, "Whose ball was that?"

Wiley answered quickly, "The ball belongs to my friend."

"But he threw it," Wilma retorted angrily.

Draw your own picture here.

_____
_____
_____
_____
_____
_____
_____
_____
_____
_____

MORE THAN ONE VIEW-POINT

Different writers and sources will give you different views of the same topic. Begin searching through different sources to see if you can find at least two different points of view on any one subject.

After you've found them, write a sentence or short paragraph summarizing each point of view. Pay special attention to the words or phrases that reflect the author's particular viewpoint.

Here are some possible sources:

poems   newspaper articles
magazine articles   magazine ads
T.V. ads   newspaper ads
billboards   newspaper headlines
history books   encyclopedias
diaries   editorials

Here are some possible topics--but you may add any of your own!

The Civil War   Fast Foods
Jogging   The Legal Driving Age
Video Movies   Rock Music
Television   Required School Attendance

DAIRY ADVERTISEMENT

MILK is good for you!
★ calcium!
★ vitamins!
★ minerals!
★ protein!

different opinions about MILK:

SCIENCE MAGAZINE

milk CAN CAUSE INDIGESTION IN BABIES!

DIET PAMPHLET

MILK IS HIGH IN FAT AND CARBOHYDRATES!

PERSONALITIES PERSONIFIED

1. Choose any four or more of the finger puppets below and on the following page to be characters in a play.
2. Write a dialogue for your play, giving the characters interesting personalities and creating an exciting plot.
3. Make your puppets (see details on next page).
4. Present your play to an audience of at least three people. Ask them to evaluate your plot for interest and originality.

Draw your own character ↑

- Have your teacher copy these figures onto card stock or paste them on tagboard to make them stronger.
- Color and cut out the figures. Wrap each around a finger and tape.
- They can be worn on your finger or moved around by themselves on a hard surface.
- You might even design a little puppet theater.

STORY-BORED? TRY STORY BOARDS!

PREPARATION:

- Ask students to bring cardboard boxes from home.
- Supply scissors, knives, markers, paints, and other art materials.

USE:

1. Have each student read a work of fiction.
2. Ask the students to draw important scenes in sequence as shown above. The back of the board may be used for showing the title, author, other books by the author, other books on the same subject, etc.
3. Provide a time when the students may look at the boards and ask each other questions.

CREATE A CARTOON

PREPARATION:
- Supply students with long, thin strips of paper (adding machine tape works nicely).

USE:
1. Ask each student to select a favorite book or story of fiction he or she has read recently, to make a list of five to ten main events from the book, and to order the events in sequence as they occurred in the book.
2. Ask the students to divide the paper strips into the number of squares needed to sequentially depict each event of the book (or story) in cartoon style (plus one square at the beginning).
3. In the first "frame", each student should write the title and author. An illustration can be added.
4. In each of the other frames, have the students write a statement describing the event and draw a cartoon illustration.

101

OUT OF ORDER

1. On a large piece of poster board or on the chalkboard, write this story (or any other story or paragraph) with the sentences in the wrong order. Include one or two ideas that do not belong in the paragraph.

EXAMPLE:

At noon he discovered he had forgotten his lunch. The bell had already rung when he got to school. His homeroom teacher's name is Mrs. Bridges. Then, at recess, he got into a fight. Everything seemed to go wrong for Rick today. His sister, Jane, is in first grade. "I certainly picked a great day for my birthday," he said to himself on the way home. The teacher had even marked him absent. In his hurry to get to school, he slipped and fell into a snowbank. First of all, he couldn't find his gloves and so he missed the bus. Half of the math period was gone, so he didn't finish the assignment.

---

2. Ask the students to rewrite the paragraph in the proper sequence, omitting the nonessentials.

WESTERN ONION SPECIAL

PREPARATION:
- Secure several copies of a blank telegram from Western Union, or create one yourself and reproduce it.

USE:
1. Show the students the format of a telegram.
2. Write some telegrams together to give the students practice in compacting their sentences and ideas.
3. Ask each student to write a summary of a library book, limiting the completed work to the space and form of a telegram. Remind them that they're paying for each word!

WESTERN ONION
BOOK-O-GRAM

NO. WORDS:	COST PER WORD:	TOTAL DUE:	CHARGE TO:	DATE:
	.25¢ p/w			19

Send To:

Address :

TITLE OF BOOK:

Sent By:

THE OTHER SIDE OF THE STORY

In most situations you will find there is more than one way to look at things. Read these situations and answer the questions.

1. ## The Story

My grandmother is so stingy. She promised to pay me $25.00 for watering her plants for this month. She only paid me $15.00, and now I can't buy the sweater I want.

Is this situation fair? _____

_____

2. ## The Story

My mom's rules are unfair! All the other kids are out skating on the rink, and here I am sitting inside.

Is this situation fair? _____

_____

1. ## The Other Side of the Story

SITUATION #1

Jenni watered the plants only once a week instead of twice as she had agreed. I hope that getting less money will help her remember next time.

Is Jenni being treated fairly?
Why?
Suggest another solution.

_____

_____

2. ## The Other Side of the Story

SITUATION #2

John's cough is much worse today and he seems to have a fever. He really needs to stay inside.

Is John being treated fairly?
Why?
Suggest another solution.

_____

_____

Turn the page upside down and answer the questions with the new information you've been given.

Now, *you* create two situations that tell one side of the story. Then turn the page over and write the other side of the story. Draw a picture for each side of each situation.

3. SITUATION #3	**4.** SITUATION #4
_____ _____ _____ _____ _____	_____ _____ _____ _____ _____

THE OTHER SIDE OF THE STORY

3.	**4.**
_____ _____ _____ _____	_____ _____ _____ _____
SITUATION #3	SITUATION #4

A Halloween Night Visitor

A HALLOWEEN NIGHT VISITOR

Being able to visualize the characters you read about is an important reading skill. To help you sharpen your powers of visualization, read the description below and draw the Halloween Night Visitor as you see him.

It was the scariest sight you could hope to see. The eerie light of the sliver, autumn moon was breathtaking. Right in the midst of gaunt and spike-like cornstalks, a head-and-a-half high, the scrawny, skeleton-like creature stood. Two eyes akin to coals of fire, a red nose, and a "mean" mouth filled with ragged teeth gave the monstrous creature a scary appearance. Could that be a gleaming steel blade clasped between his teeth? The tall, black hat with a ragged brim and feather added to his spooky presence. A wooly muffler made of some unfathomable plaid, a jacket two sizes too large, somber black trousers, a torn shirt and gym shoes beyond repair completed the mysterious fellow's attire.

NOT AN ORDINARY MORNING

Read the story and finish the last sentence with a surprise ending. Illustrate the story on the back of this page to show the scene. Include all the details that Susan saw from her bedroom window.

Susan awoke with the feeling that something very special had taken place while she was sleeping. She jumped out of bed and rushed to the window. She could hardly believe her eyes. The entire ground was completely covered with snow. The trees and bushes looked as if they had been painted by an artist using only white paint and a giant brush. Even the tracks made by the paper boy on his early morning rounds were covered. Not a creature was moving. The stillness and quiet were almost eerie. In all of Susan's life it had never snowed this far south. As she was turning from the window she saw...

OH, MOTHER!

1. Read the description Mrs. Merry Monthofmay's daughter wrote about her mother.
2. Then, draw and color a full-length portrait of Mrs. Merry Monthofmay to be hung in the local art gallery.
3. After you have completed your portrait, go back and underline the key words or phrases that caused you to visualize Mrs. Merry Monthofmay as you did.

She is a fun-loving, cheerful lady. Her curly red hair, green eyes, rosy red cheeks, long, curly eyelashes, and cheerful smile are the features one notices first. The fact that she dresses in clothes one size too large or too small, always from a flea market or tag sale, seems of little importance. Ragged tennis shoes, mismatched athletic socks, and a dozen or so jangling bracelets often complete her attire. The oversized carpet bag that she carries contains lollipops for the kids she knows, old paperback books for friends and neighbors, bags of freshly baked cookies, and a collection of goodies from the five-and-dime store to be distributed to anyone down in the dumps. She always wears a flower in her hair—sometimes a real one, but oftentimes the biggest, most colorful artificial one she can find. She is my mother.

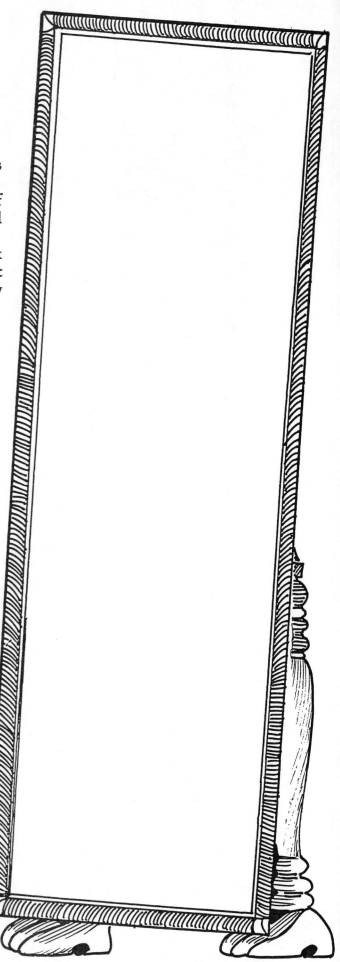

WRITING

WORDS ON WHEELS

PREPARATION:
- Gather colored poster board, crayons or markers, and scissors.

USE:
1. Ask the students to think of words that can be used as substitutes for the word **pretty**. Make a list of their suggestions.
2. Talk about some other words that are commonly overused such as **said, walked, then, happy, funny, asked, cute,** etc. Compile your own class list of such overused words.
3. Have the students work alone or in pairs. Ask them to choose an "overworked" word and to make a WORD WHEEL. The word becomes the hub of the wheel and the alternative words become the spokes. Encourage the students to use interesting alternative words and to decorate the wheels attractively.
4. Mount the finished wheels on the wall to make a permanent thesaurus for your writers. Whenever they are writing and want to use one of the overused words, they may look at the wall and choose a more specific or more interesting word.

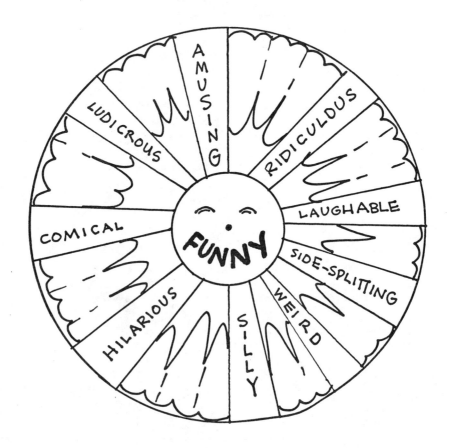

BROWN BAG MYSTERIES

PREPARATION:
- Fill a small paper bag for each student with one object such as:

cotton ball	sticker	rubber band
small toy car	plastic ball	straw
flower	shoelace	cookie
watch	stamp	mitten
small scissors	sock	eraser
tweezers	carrot	feather
jackknife	bow	belt buckle

- Ahead of time, write short descriptions of several items other than the ones above, each time omitting the name of the item. Put the items in bags and attach the descriptions to the outside.

USE:
1. After reading a description, ask the students to guess the mystery item.
2. Repeat the same procedure with one or two other items.
3. Discuss the kinds of clues given in the descriptions that helped the listeners solve the mysteries.
4. Give each student a bag and ask him or her to write a clever description of the mystery item without giving away the item's name.
5. Have them attach the written descriptions to the bags and then trade bags to guess the contents.

NOW YOU SEE IT, NOW YOU DON'T

PREPARATION:
- Prepare a mounted assortment of interesting pictures from magazines.
- Write a clear description for two pictures.

USE:
1. Ask the students to close their eyes and listen as you read one of the descriptions. (Do not show the picture.) Tell them to let a picture form in their minds as you read.
2. Then, show them the picture. Talk about how it compares to their visual images. Discuss what the writer did well and what could have been done to make the description more accurate.
3. Repeat the process with another picture.
4. Give each student a picture (covered so others can't see it), and ask the student to write a description.
5. Have them trade descriptions so that each can draw the picture he or she "sees" after reading someone else's written description.
6. Compare the drawings to the original pictures. Allow time for the writers to discuss the results with the persons who drew the pictures.

DON'T BE AFRAID OF BIG WORDS!

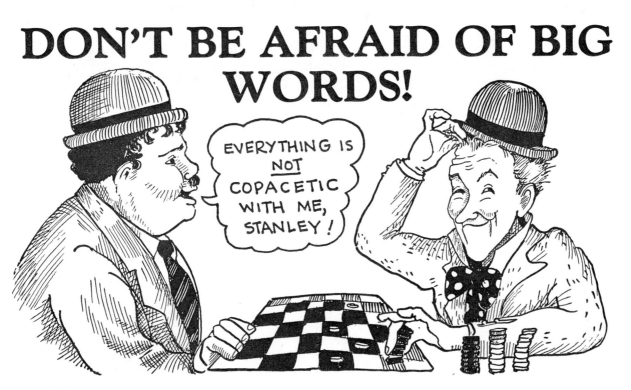

Big words can be a lot of fun!

Choose one of the words below (or find one on your own). Write a paragraph describing what the word seems to mean. Include an explanation of the real meaning, too. (See the example.)

COPACETIC – you say it like this: KO (rhymes with toe)-pa-set-ik

It could be a medicine you'd put on a cut finger or a scraped knee, don't you think?

Actually, the soothing sound of copacetic does give you a clue to its real meaning. It has a smooth, easy, agreeable sound. And that's what it means – that everything is okay. When you want to tell someone that all is just fine with you, you say, "I'm Copacetic!"

obstreperous
accouterments
palindrome
tatterdemalion
pandiculation
tourniquet

lachrymose
abecedarian
amaranthine
saponaceous
architectural
perpendicular

113

RHINOCEROS FOR SALE

CLASSIFIEDS . . . .

LIQUIDATION SALE

1969 Calendar/diary
—hardly used.
fly swatter (broken
handle.)
"Tiny Tim" record col-
lection—COMPLETE!
Accordion—(needs
tuning.)
Six Cartons rubber
bands —never
used

SKIS OFFERED, brand
new. Only used once.
HALF PRICE. Call
555-4400 evenings.
ASK FOR "PEG-LEG?"

WANTED: DEPE?!
YOUNGSTER TO V?
MY DOG AFTER?:.
$2.50 per hour ?? ··
555- 7963

RHINOCEROS FOR SALE
SLIGHTLY USED RHINO. Mild tempered,
housebroken, friendly to animals and
children. Good condition.
Best offer. 555-0900

Read some classified ads in your local newspaper. Notice that each ad gives a pretty complete description of the item for sale but uses very few words. That's because you pay by the word for the ad.

You need to sell each of the items shown. Write a classified ad for each one. Include all the information necessary to interest buyers. But remember, each word costs 25¢, so keep it short. You only have $5.00 for each ad.

UNICYCLE

RO-
BOT

CAMERA

YOUR CHOICE

YOU'RE BEING FOLLOWED!

PREPARATION:

- Have ready several pieces of paper which can be inserted into a loose-leaf binder.

USE:

1. When introducing students to the skill of developing a character in a piece of writing, work with them to collect a general list of each of the following. You will need to continue this for two or three days. Put the lists in a binder.

   - words that describe various appearances
   - attributes of personality
   - activities, actions, jobs, professions
   - words that describe body language or movements
   - feelings you have about different people
   - unusual or memorable habits
   - positive qualities
   - negative or irritating qualities or habits
   - words and phrases that describe attitudes

2. Ask each student to choose one person to "follow" over the next several days. It may be anyone whom the student sees often. The students are to collect bits of information about the people they follow, similar to the kinds of ideas collected in class, and are to write the information in a notebook. You might give them a list identical to the one above. Instruct the students to write at least one short anecdote about their chosen persons.

3. When they bring their notes back to class, give them time to organize their information into interesting tales or character descriptions. Make available to the students the list of words they collected earlier (see #1) to help them in developing the characters' personalities.

GAME OF THE NAME

TOMORROW'S AIR SHOW
RESCHEDULED AGAIN!!

These kids have used the letters of their names to make headlines for a news story.

BILL: Bear In Local Laundry

NANCY: "Never Allow Nukes", Congressman Yells

JIM: Jury Is Mute

SARA: Seven Aunts Raise Alligators

MY NAME:_____

You do the same with yours!

Now write a news article to go with your name headline.

(headline)_____

_____

_____

_____

_____

_____

_____

_____

_____

_____

NEWSWORTHY FAIRY TALES

RED R. HOOD POSES WITH RESCUER AT THE SCENE OF THE INCIDENT.

WOODCUTTER RESCUES GIRL FROM WOLF

(Red Forest, Cal., UPI) Mr. I. Cut Wood was awarded a medal of bravery for his quick and courageous action in saving the life of a young girl yesterday. Mr. Wood was chopping trees three miles east of this northern California town when he heard screams. He responded to the cries and entered a cottage at 482 Country Lane where he found 10-year-old Red R. Hood being mauled by a wolf. Wood overpowered the animal with his axe in a matter of minutes.

According to Mrs. Agatha Hood, grandmother of the girl and owner of the dwelling, the wolf forcibly entered the dwelling about 2:30 p.m. The wolf allegedly snatched Mrs. Hood's bonnet, locked her in a closet, and awaited the arrival of the granddaughter. Mrs. Hood said she could hear conversation taking place between the wolf and her granddaughter before the screams began.

The young Miss Hood was treated for scrapes and bruises at the Captain Hook Memorial Hospital and later was released to the care of her parents, Mr. and Mrs. Amos Hood of 2694 Rapunzel Lane.

Both the SPCA and the FRIENDS of WILD ANIMALS SOCIETY have indicated they plan to file suit against Mr. Wood for cruel and unnecessary slaughter of the wolf, a member of an endangered species. A hearing is slated for next Thursday.

PREPARATION:
- Have available a list of familiar fairy tales and an assortment of newspaper headlines and articles.

USE:
1. Write a list of familiar fairy tale titles on the chalkboard. Briefly review each tale with the students.
2. Choose one fairy tale. Ask the students to imagine how it might read as a news article in today's newspaper.
3. Have the students look over several recent news articles to find the kinds of words and phrases used to describe events in the stories and headlines.
4. Brainstorm for headlines for the tale. Then work together to create a news account of the fairy tale.
5. After they've practiced with the group, let the students work alone or in small groups to turn another fairy tale into a current news article.

STRICTLY PRIVATE

JOURNALS are a wonderful way for students to increase skills while they benefit from the freedom of private writing. It's a great way to write on all sorts of topics, without the risk of having to share with or please anyone else.

PREPARATION:
- Each student (and teacher) needs a notebook.
- The teacher needs a list of ideas to suggest.

USE:
1. Provide private writing time of 5-20 minutes as often as possible.
2. Suggest a topic for writing (see examples, and/or let individuals write what they wish).
3. Declare the journals off limits to everyone but the individual authors. (Students may wish to let the teacher look at their journals now and then.)
4. Encourage the students to try many different forms of writing (poems, paragraphs, questions, stories, etc.), and to use their journals for gathering ideas.
5. During the writing time, write in *your* journal, too.
6. Share some of your entries and encourage, but don't force, the students to do the same.
7. Journals can be used later as the basis for writing lessons. For instance, you might ask students periodically to choose an entry from their journals which they will develop and polish into a completed piece of writing for publishing or sharing.
8. Journals are not intended to be corrected mechanically, except when students are working to polish an entry.

You'll be surprised at how much your writers will develop when they're given so much pressure-free time to write.

Suggested directions and topics for JOURNAL WRITING

Morning feelings
Dreams
Wishes
Disappointments
Protests
Weather
Close encounters
Future plans
Mistakes
Opinions
Hostilities

Joys
Pains
Compliments
Fears
Memories
Worries
Sounds/noises
Past regrets
Exciting experiences
Dilemmas
Secrets

Who Am I?
Descriptions of important events
Diary-style recounts of the day
Notes to teachers
Letters to God
Things you'd like to say to someone but are afraid to say
People I like
People I don't like
A person I would like to know better
A person who puzzles (irritates, intrigues, attracts) me

Things I'd like to change . . .
I wish I knew . . .
When I was little . . .
Places I wish I could visit . . .
Places I never want to visit . . .
If I could do it over . . .
Adventures I'd like to have . . .
Today I'm thinking about . . .
I wonder why . . .
If only . . .
I never could do without . . .
It isn't fair . . .

ATTENTION! ATTENTION!

PREPARATION:

● Write and post one or more announcements for actual events of interest to your students.

USE:

1. Give or show the announcement(s) to your class.
2. Talk about the purpose of announcements. Have the students help to generate a list of the important ingredients of an effective announcement. For example:

  ● information given clearly, concisely
  ● who is sponsoring or conducting
  ● exact time, date, place, cost
  ● what the event is
  ● who may participate or did participate
  ● how long it lasted or will last
  ● requirements for involvement

3. Ask students to create an announcement for one of the following past, present, or future events (others may be added):

  the arrival of a queen
  an act in a talent show
  a writing contest
  a race of pet snakes
  an upcoming T.V. show
  the results of a recent sports event
  their own births
  a recent or upcoming visitation by beings from another planet
  a surprise party for the principal
  the cancellation of a test

4. Students may create a written poster to make the announcement or prepare a written script to read to the class.

TALL, TALL TALES

PREPARATION:
- Find a collection of tall tales in your library. (A book of American folklore will have some.)
- Have on hand: 11 x 18 inch black construction paper, adding machine tape (2 inches or wider), scissors, and glue.

USE:
1. Read a few tall tales to the students.
2. Take turns telling your own tall tales (lies or exaggerated stories).
3. Build a list of the kinds of topics that lend themselves well to stretched stories.
4. Let each student write a rough draft of his or her own tall tale.
5. When the students are ready to make the final drafts, have them write on long strips of adding machine tape to make "tall" stories.
6. Paste the finished tales on long strips of black construction paper. Have the students cut and attach long, long legs and hats to their tales to make them really tall.
7. Display the tall, tall tales on a wall or bulletin board.

MY TALL TALE IS ABOUT

GETTING THERE FROM HERE

Choose any TWO spots on the map. Write them here:

A _____ B _____

Write clear, step-by-step directions for getting from A to B.

_____

_____

_____

_____

_____

_____

_____

Now, review the directions to make sure they are correct.

Then, give these directions and the map to a friend. See if he or she can get to the right spot by following your directions.

If not, fix the directions to make them accurate.

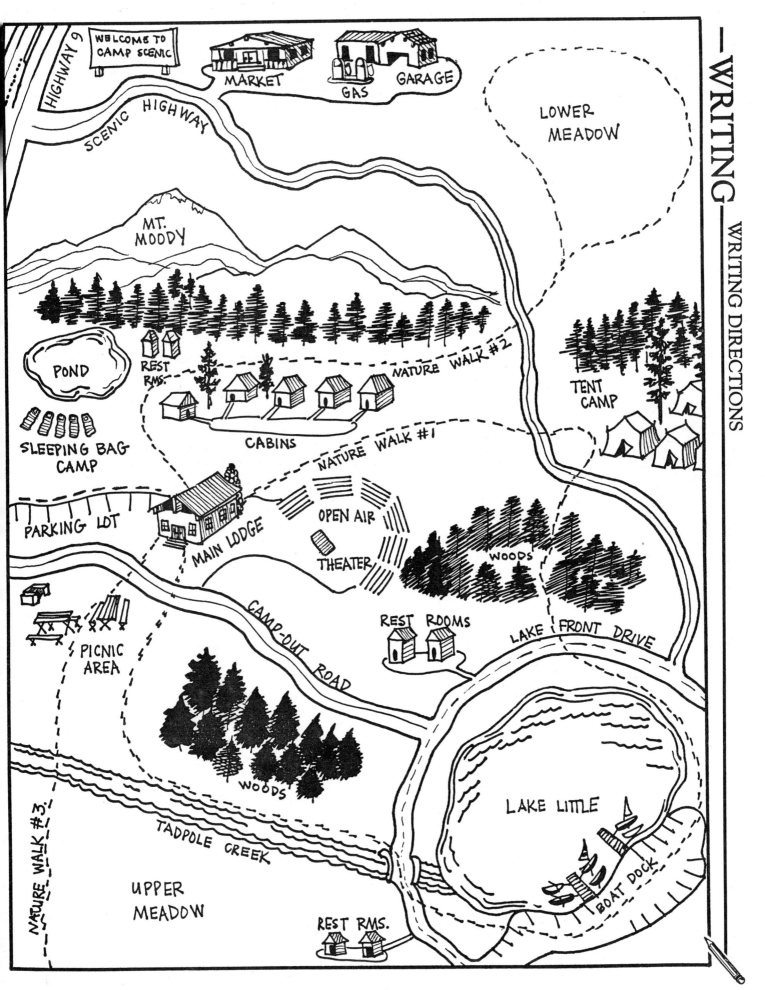

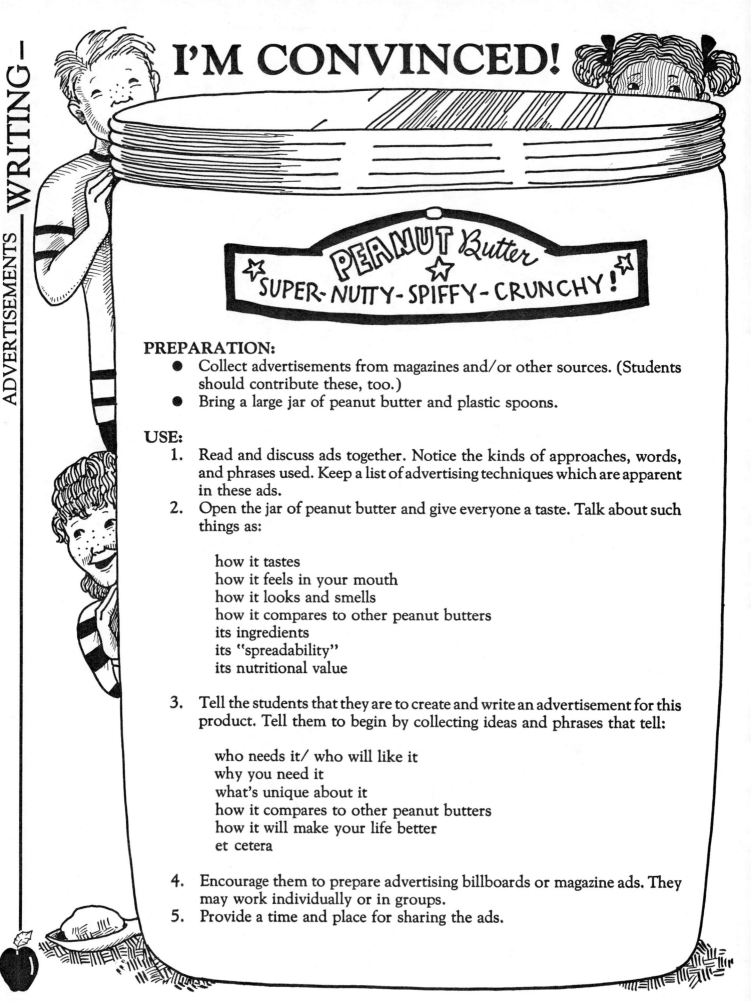

I'M CONVINCED!

PEANUT Butter
☆ SUPER- NUTTY- SPIFFY- CRUNCHY! ☆

PREPARATION:
- Collect advertisements from magazines and/or other sources. (Students should contribute these, too.)
- Bring a large jar of peanut butter and plastic spoons.

USE:

1. Read and discuss ads together. Notice the kinds of approaches, words, and phrases used. Keep a list of advertising techniques which are apparent in these ads.

2. Open the jar of peanut butter and give everyone a taste. Talk about such things as:

   how it tastes
   how it feels in your mouth
   how it looks and smells
   how it compares to other peanut butters
   its ingredients
   its "spreadability"
   its nutritional value

3. Tell the students that they are to create and write an advertisement for this product. Tell them to begin by collecting ideas and phrases that tell:

   who needs it/ who will like it
   why you need it
   what's unique about it
   how it compares to other peanut butters
   how it will make your life better
   et cetera

4. Encourage them to prepare advertising billboards or magazine ads. They may work individually or in groups.

5. Provide a time and place for sharing the ads.

IT'S YOUR BUSINESS

```
1132 King Way
Busytown, Maine   07691
May 3, 1986


Joe's Pizza Place
1473 Main Street
Busytown, Maine   07691

Dear Sir:

Our family really enjoys your
"The Works" pizza.  We are
wondering if you would be
willing to share the recipe
with us.  If so, we'd appreciate
your sending it to the above
address.

Thank you.

Yours truly,

John Wilson

John Wilson
```

Review the form for a business letter. Ask your teacher for plain paper, a business envelope, and a phone book.

Write a real letter to someone in your town or city. (Businesses or government agencies will often answer you.)

Here are some ideas. Use the phone book to get other ideas and to find addresses. (You may need a zip code directory, too.)

```
John Wilson
1132 King Way
Busytown, Maine   07691


                        Joe's Pizza Place
                        1473 Main Street
                        Busytown, Maine 07691
```

Write to:

- An Italian restaurant, asking if they'll share a recipe for their spaghetti sauce
- Your mayor, telling her or him how you feel about something related to your town or city
- The telephone company, asking how they arrive at their phone rates
- A dairy, asking for any free publications they may have for schools
- The school superintendent, asking him or her to tell you what is important about a good education
- A sporting goods store, requesting leftover sports posters for your classroom
- A newspaper, asking them to describe necessary qualifications for being a reporter on their staff
- A bicycle repair shop, inquiring about their fee for a new tire
- The state Motor Vehicles Division, requesting a free copy of the manual to study for a driver's license
- OR . . . look in the yellow pages and come up with your own ideas!

Write a rough copy of your letter, check it for mistakes, and copy it on a clean sheet. (You might have your teacher look it over, too.) Address the envelope, put a stamp on it, mail it, and wait for an answer!

FROM Bach TO ROCK

PREPARATION:
- You will need several selections of music, on tapes or records, and a tape recorder and/or record player.
- Arrange a comfortable spot for students to listen to music.

USE:
1. With students relaxing in a comfortable listening position, play a piece of music from beginning to end.
2. Play it again with the volume down a little. This time brainstorm ideas, words and phrases with the help of suggestions and questions such as:

   "What does the music make you feel like doing?"
   "What pictures come to your mind?"
   "Let's collect some words that fit this music."
   "What feelings do you have about this music?"
   "What kind of setting does this bring to mind?"

3. Repeat this process with another piece of music.
4. With a third piece, start collecting words, phrases and impressions in writing (on the board or overhead projector).
5. Play the third piece again and ask the students to write a few paragraphs, a description, a poem, a story, or any other piece of writing that "matches" the music.

WHAT FEELING DO YOU GET FROM THIS MUSIC?

SOUND SEARCH

Where would you hear these sounds? (You can write more than one place.)

gurgling and slurping _____

a shriek of delight _____

crunch, crunch _____

crisp snapping _____

roaring, pounding water _____

a warm sigh _____

a low, hungry growl _____

a melancholy wail _____

angry muttering _____

rhythmic electronic beeps _____

What might you hear here? (Write two phrases for each place.)

shopping mall _____ , _____

waterslide _____ , _____

hospital _____ , _____

church _____ , _____

bookstore _____ , _____

zoo _____ , _____

Visit one of these places and listen carefully for sounds. Write several phrases (two or more words) describing the sounds.

cafeteria	gym	office	hallway
kitchen	playground	library	another classroom

_____

_____

_____

SIMPLY DELICIOUS

Which of these descriptions is more appealing to you?

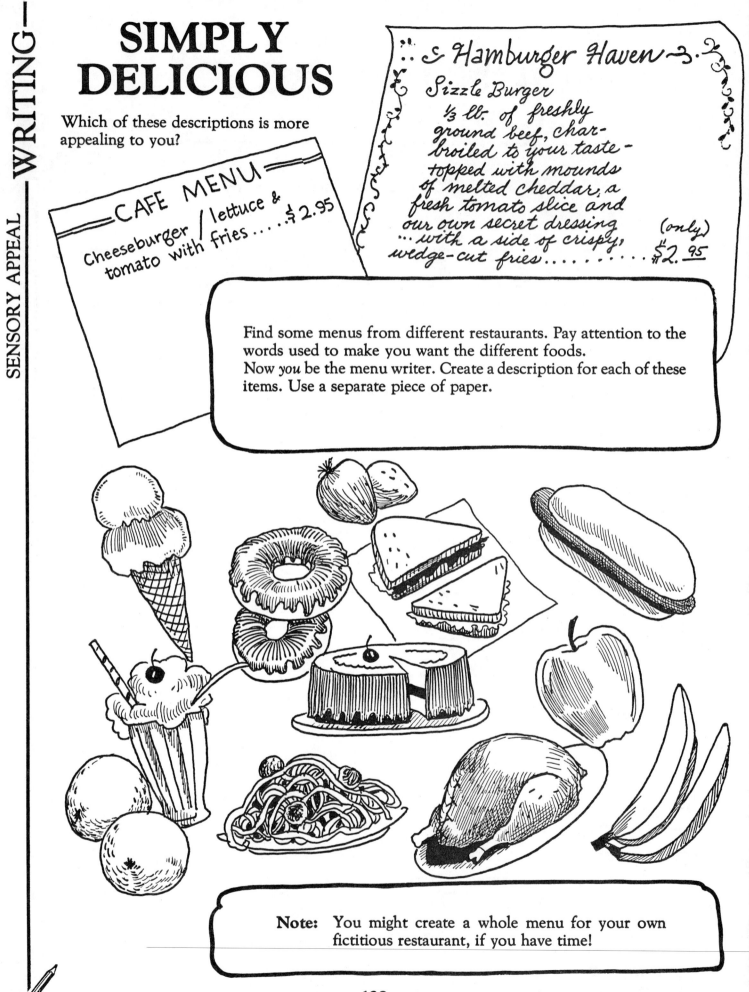

CAFE MENU

Cheeseburger / lettuce & tomato with fries.....$2.95

~~ Hamburger Haven ~~

Sizzle Burger

⅓ lb. of freshly ground beef, char-broiled to your taste - topped with mounds of melted cheddar, a fresh tomato slice and our own secret dressing ... with a side of crispy, wedge-cut fries..........

(only) $2.95

Find some menus from different restaurants. Pay attention to the words used to make you want the different foods.

Now *you* be the menu writer. Create a description for each of these items. Use a separate piece of paper.

Note: You might create a whole menu for your own fictitious restaurant, if you have time!

BEHIND THE MASK

PREPARATION:

- Gather a supply of lightweight poster board in a variety of colors, scissors, glue, markers or paints, and other "decorations" to add to masks (such as feathers, sequins, fabric scraps, yarn, ribbon, etc.). Also provide a tongue depressor or short wooden stick for each student.

USE:

DAY 1 Discuss how faces reveal different feelings and emotions. Students might practice making their own faces show emotions such as:

fear	confusion	disappointment
joy	surprise	jealousy
anger	excitement	sadness
pain	frustration	embarrassment
regret	shock	anxiety

Have each student design and create a mask which shows one emotion.

DAY 2 Together, collect some words and phrases that effectively express the various emotions discussed.
Let each student develop a long list of words and phrases specifically for his or her mask.

DAY 3 Give the students time to write about a situation which communicates the emotion shown by his or her mask.

DAY 4 When the writing is done, provide a way to share or display the writing and the masks.

COOL AS A CUCUMBER

Read one of the following similies to the class. (Each one is completed in the most frequently used manner.)

Give the students five minutes to write at least one different ending for the simile (ie: "cool as a mountain waterfall" or "cool as an angry stare"). Brainstorm to encourage unusual, fresh similes.

Fresh as . . . a daisy.
Good as . . . gold.
Sweet as . . . sugar.
Clear as . . . a bell.
Quick as . . . a wink.
Clean as . . . a whistle.
Neat as . . . a pin.
Blind as . . . a bat.
Cool as . . . a cucumber.
Stubborn as . . . a mule.
Dead as . . . a doornail.
Pale as . . . a ghost.
Light as . . . a feather.
Pretty as . . . a picture.
Funny as . . . a clown.
Poor as . . . a church mouse.
Soft as . . . cotton.
Rich as . . . a king.
Sneaky as . . . a thief.
Quiet as . . . a mouse.
Wiggly as . . . a worm.

A DUCK IS LIKE A STOMACH-ACHE?

A metaphor is a way of speaking that suggests a likeness between two things or two ideas which are not usually seen as being alike.

Make some original metaphors by finishing these:

A duck is like a stomachache because _____ .

I am like _____ because _____ .

Anger is like _____ because _____ .

Losing a friend is as _____ as riding a Ferris wheel.

_____ is as confusing as tangled shoelaces.

A principal is like a vacuum cleaner because _____

_____ .

A smile is louder than a frown because _____

_____ .

_____ is like _____ because they both hurt a long time.

_____ is like standing on top of a volcano.

_____ is like _____ because they both have a surprise in them.

A goldfish is as _____ as a math test.

Pain is heavier than _____ because _____ .

131

IT FIGURES!

Figures of speech are expressions used to convey meaning or to heighten the effect of the writing. Here are a few.

Alliteration--the repetition of beginning consonant sounds
(Silly Sarah sewed seventeen stitches in her sister.)

Onomatopoeia--naming something with a word that makes the sound associated with it
(buzz, hiss, crash, crunch, fizz, sizzle)

Personification--giving personal qualities to a nonhuman thing
(The alarm clock maliciously clobbered me with its bell.)

Hyperbole--extreme exaggeration
(There must be a million people on this bus.)

Write a figure of speech for each picture. Use each figure of speech at least once. Label each one A, O, P, or H.

MIXED-UP MOTHER GOOSE

What if Jack Horner got stuck running up a clock, or Peter Pumpkin Eater's wife tried to jump over a candlestick in her pumpkin? How would the nursery rhymes be changed?

JACK and JILL WENT UP THE HILL TO FETCH A PAIL OF WATER, A SPIDER CLIMBED UP AFTER JILL, SHE RAN, BUT THE SPIDER CAUGHT HER.

Choose any two or more of these (or other) nursery rhymes and combine them into a new one. (You can write on the back of this page.)

Baa Baa Black Sheep
Hey Diddle Diddle
Jack, Be Nimble
Little Miss Muffet
Old King Cole
Old Mother Hubbard
Rub-A-Dub-Dub
Wee Willie Winkie
Simple Simon
Georgy Porgy
Humpty Dumpty
Hickory Dickory Dock
Diddle Diddle Dumpling
Fe, Fi, Fo, Fum
Jack Sprat Could Eat No Fat
Little Boy Blue
London Bridge Is Falling Down
Peter Pumpkin Eater
Peter Piper Picked A Peck

Be sure to draw a picture to accompany your finished rhyme!

A DIAMOND OF OPPOSITES

HOT

Steamy, Humid

Sizzling, Sticky, sweating,

SUMMER, SUN, WINTER, ICE,

chattering, Shivering, Freezing

Chilly, Frigid

COLD

WHAT YOU NEED:
- A list of antonym pairs (see your teacher), poster board, scissors, glue, magazines.

WHAT TO DO:
1. The following is an example of a **diamante**, or diamond poem. Pay special attention to the form (outlined below).
2. Choose a pair of opposites and write your own **diamante** of opposites.

1 _____   (first opposite)

2 _____ , _____   (2 adjectives describing first opposite)

3 _____ , _____ , _____   (3 participles describing first opposite)

4 ____ , ____ , ____ , ____ (2 nouns related to first line, 2 related to its opposite)

5 _____ , _____ , _____   (3 participles describing second opposite)

6 _____ , _____   (2 adjectives describing second opposite)

7 _____   (second opposite)

3. When your **diamante** is finished, write it on a diamond-shaped piece of paper. Then, cut pictures which show each opposite from magazines. Make a collage mounted on a diamond-shaped piece of poster board. Display your **diamante** on this collage.

ORIGINAL EPITAPHS

1959-1979
HERE LIES
JONATHON McMURG
AT LAST HE'S FREE
FROM DOING
HOMEWORK

HERE LIES UNCLE BEN
WHO TOOK A NAP
IN A LION'S DEN—
1840-1902

R.I.P.
HERE LIES TEENAGER JOAN
SHE STARVED TO DEATH
TALKING ON THE PHONE!
1970-1984

ELLIE McNat
1969-1981
Farewell to friend,
Ellie McNat
Life is dangerous for
an acrobat.

POOR OLD ZELDA ZATT
WENT FOR A SWIM
IN A PICKLE VAT
1920-1984

FAREWELL,
FAREWELL
to mischievous
MICHAEL
He shouldn't
have toyed
with that
motorcycle!
1970-
1985

An **epitaph** is a short statement written on a tomb in memory of the person buried there.
Epitaphs don't have to rhyme, but it's fun to write ones that do.

Finish these:

DANGEROUS DAN LIES IN
PEACE

got a French fry
stuck in his
throat!

FAREWELL TO OUR DEAR, RICH,
FRIEND, SONNY

HERE RESTS
WILLIAM BROWN

!

MOUNTAIN CLIMBER MARTHA
LIES BELOW

HE DIED from BEING SUCH A GROUCH

Farewell to Ballerina Nell

IF SHE'D BEEN SMART, SHE'D HAVE STAYED IN SCHOOL!

MISERABLE
Poor Old ↓ Matt

1913 — 1986

Her Mother warned her not to lie

Now, do these from beginning to end. Don't forget the name and date at the top.

QUITE A QUIZAINE

PREPARATION:
- Gather a selection of 11 x 17 inch colored construction paper, glue, scissors, markers, crayons.

> *Grown-ups hurry all the time.*
> *Does life go faster*
> *As you age?*

USE:

1. A **quizaine** is a special kind of poem that asks a question. Notice the form:

    Line 1 makes a statement, 2 and 3 ask a question.

    (Line 1) 7 syllables
    (Line 2) 5 syllables
    (Line 3) 3 syllables

2. Start a discussion with the students about questions. Start them talking about some of the things they'd like to know about the world, how things work, or why things happen. Generate a list of some of their ideas.
3. Share a few **quizaines** with them, pointing out the form.
4. Work together to write a couple of **quizaines**. Then ask the students to try some on their own.
5. Have the students cut large question marks from construction paper. They may decorate them and write or mount their quizaines on them for display.

WEATHERGRAMS

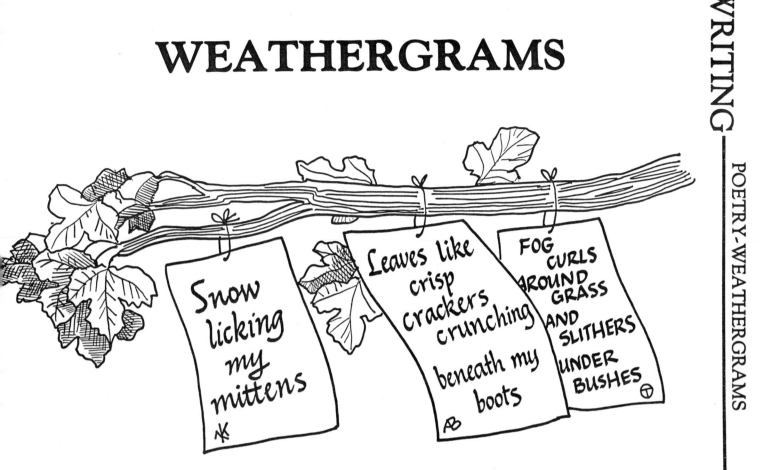

A **weathergram** is a very short poem (10 words or less) on the subject of nature, made with all natural materials. After writing the poem, hang it outside where it can be finished by the wind, rain, snow and sun. In about three months it becomes a true **weathergram**.

PREPARATION:
- Collect brown grocery bags, scissors, a hole punch, thin jute twine, permanent ink, and dip pens.
- Make one or more **weathergrams** to show the students.

USE:
1. Show a weathergram to the students and explain what it is.
2. Take the students on a walk or on an outdoor adventure to gather ideas for weathergrams. Brainstorm for ideas and keep a list of good nature-related topics.
3. Outdoors (if weather permits) or indoors, let the students write their own weathergrams.
4. Cut a 2½ by 10 inch piece of paper for each weathergram. Fold two inches back at the top, punch out a hole, and thread the hole with a loop of twine.
5. Then, using permanent ink, students may write their poems in handwriting or calligraphy. Each student should add a sign or symbol that is his or her personal mark (instead of signing his or her name).
6. Finally, each student may hang the weathergram in a natural setting where passers-by can enjoy the brief poem. A tree or bush in a backyard, along a trail, or in the woods would be good. The weathergrams will not mar the scenery and are completely decomposable.

LET'S LIMERICK

This poem is a **limerick**:

> *A lady who was smelling a rose*
> *Found a parakeet perched on her nose.*
> *The rose made her sneeze*
> *Which buckled her knees*
> *Now the parakeet sits on her toes.*

Notice that the five-lined **limerick** follows this pattern:

Line 1	States the situation
Line 2	Tells what happened
Lines 3,4	Tells what went wrong
Line 5	So what! (or, what happened then)

Notice also the rhyme pattern:

Lines 1,2,5	rhyme
Lines 3,4	rhyme

Now, are you ready to write some limericks? Let's get started by finishing these:

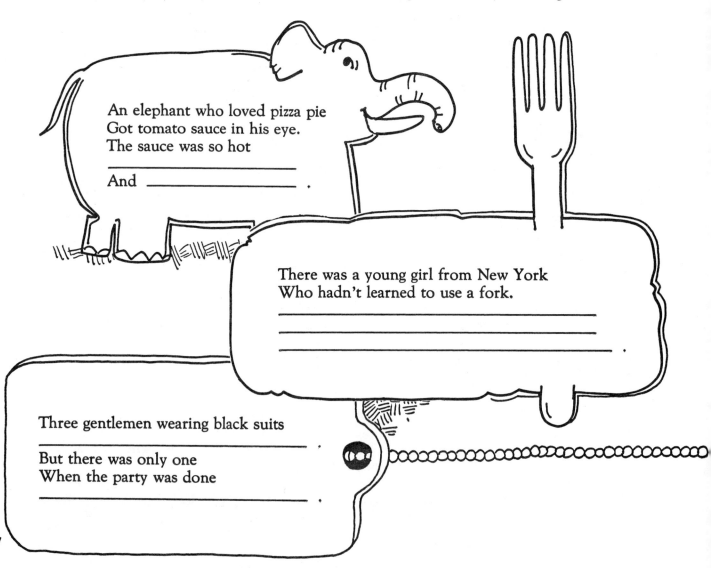

An elephant who loved pizza pie
Got tomato sauce in his eye.
The sauce was so hot

_____

And _____ .

There was a young girl from New York
Who hadn't learned to use a fork.

_____

_____

_____ .

Three gentlemen wearing black suits

_____ .

But there was only one
When the party was done

_____ .

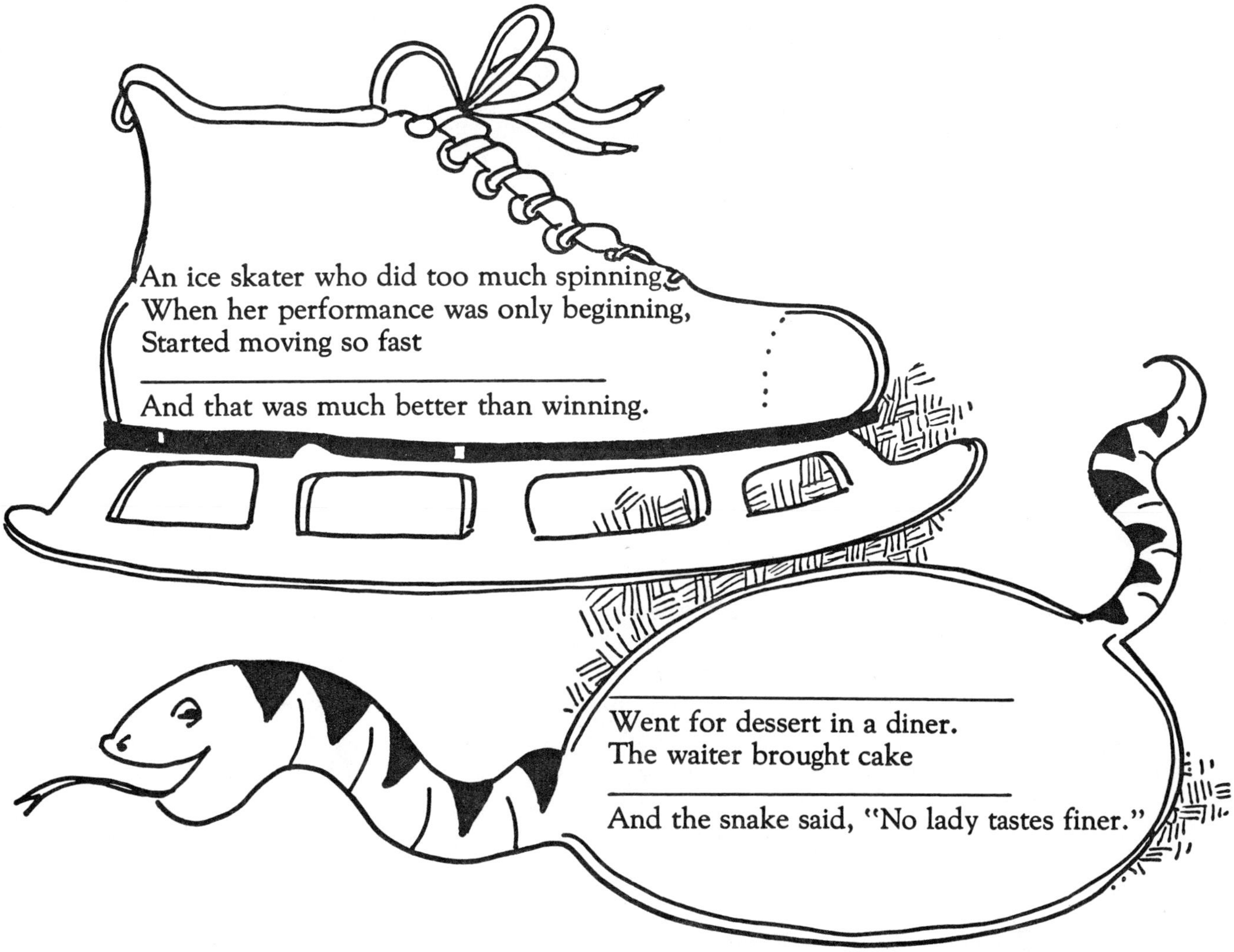

An ice skater who did too much spinning,
When her performance was only beginning,
Started moving so fast

_____

And that was much better than winning.

_____

Went for dessert in a diner.
The waiter brought cake

_____

And the snake said, "No lady tastes finer."

Now write one or two of your own! (You can illustrate them.)
_____ (Title)

_____

_____

_____

_____

_____

_____ (Title)

_____

_____

_____

_____

_____

141

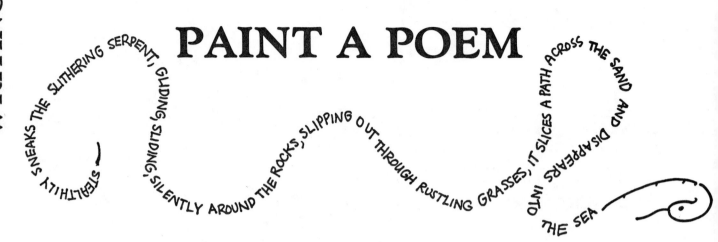

PAINT A POEM

STEALTHILY SNEAKS THE SLITHERING SERPENT, GLIDING, SLIDING, SILENTLY AROUND THE ROCKS, SLIPPING OUT THROUGH RUSTLING GRASSES, IT SLICES A PATH ACROSS THE SAND AND DISAPPEARS INTO THE SEA

This is called a **painted** poem because the words are written on the paper in a shape or design that shows what the poem is about.

1. Think of other topics for painted poems. Here's a start:

    a bouncing ball   fireworks   ocean waves
    a tornado   a flock of birds   the wind

    _____

    _____

2. Choose one topic for your painted poem.
3. Collect some words and phrases about that topic.

    _____

    _____

    _____

    _____

    _____

    _____

4. Combine your ideas into a poem. Write it on a separate piece of paper.
5. When you are satisfied with your poem, take a blank piece of white drawing paper and write your poem in a *painted* shape. Print each word large so that your shape fills the paper nicely.
6. Finally, use colored chalk or crayon to add color to your painted design. This will make it look smashing!

FRAMED FAVORITES

PREPARATION:
- Gather cardboard, paints, markers, scissors, glue, and other supplies for making frames.

USE:

DAY 1 Give the students time to make interesting, decorative frames which will be used for showing off their favorite words. Encourage a variety of shapes and kinds of frames. (You make one, too.) Insert plain paper in the opening of the frame.

DAY 2 Have the students write at least five words in the frame. These should be words they like.

DAYS 3, 4, 5
Instruct the students to add at least two words each day to their frames.

ANY DAYS THEREAFTER
Use the frames as the "raw material" for a number of writing assignments, ie:
- Choose five words that start with the same sound and put them into an alliterative sentence.
- Make one word a candidate in an election for the "world's greatest word". Write a campaign speech convincing people to vote for the word.
- Write dictionary entries for 15 of your words. Arrange them alphabetically to make a mini-dictionary.

TASTY WORDS

PREPARATION:
- Provide an apple for each student.

USE:

1. Pass out apples to the students. Ask them to feel, smell, touch, and look carefully at the apples (no tasting, yet).

2. Begin to collect words and phrases that describe the apple. Instruct the students as follows:

   "Write two words that tell how it looks."
   "Write a smell word."
   "Write some words that describe how it feels."

3. Ask the students to take a bite. As they eat, instruct them as follows:

   "Write a taste word."
   "How does it feel in your mouth? Write a phrase."
   "Write an 'aftertaste' word."
   "How does it sound when you bite and chew?"
   "Write a phrase that describes the sound of the group chewing apples."

4. Add similes and metaphors to the collection.

   This apple reminds me of _____ .
   My apple is as juicy as _____ .
   This apple is as chewy as _____ .
   I'd rather eat apples than _____ .

5. You may stop the activity after the ideas are collected, or you may have each student write a paragraph or poem about apples.

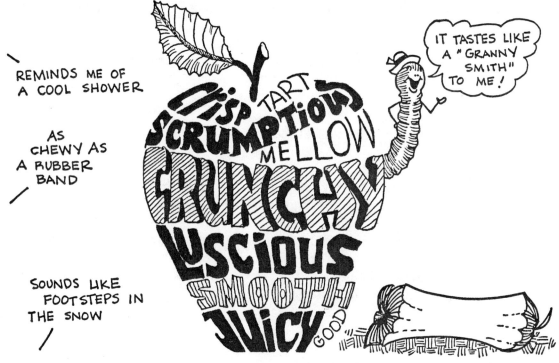

144

IT'S THAT SIMPLE

Choose an activity that you know how to do and that you can teach to others.

Ideas: How to tie your shoe   How to blow a bubble
           How to make a milkshake   How to eat spaghetti
           How to change a tire   How to make a videotape

Write your idea here: HOW TO _____

Write all the steps that need to be followed:

_____

_____

_____

_____

_____

Are your steps in the right order?
Have you included each step?
Follow your own directions to make
   sure they are clear and complete.
Make any corrections or changes.

Write your corrected outline below.

....

          (Title) _____

I. _____

II. _____

III. _____

IV. _____

V. _____

VI. _____

Cut out your outline to use as a guide, and be ready to give a "how-to-do-it" speech to the class.

EASY AS A-B-C

ALPHABET TALES and **POEMS** are such fun to write. And they're pretty easy, too!

Here's how you do it:

1. Choose ONE letter of the alphabet. _____
2. Write a list of interesting words beginning with that letter, and some phrases which have several words in them beginning with that letter. Use the dictionary to help you find new or unusual words.
    Use the back of this paper to build your list. Work on it over a period of a few days.
3. Next, spend a couple of days putting some of the words and phrases together into a good sentence, story, joke, or poem.
4. Cut, design, and decorate a huge, poster board letter to display your finished **ALPHABET TALE**. Write or mount your final copy on the letter.

I'm Jeremy Jake of the jolly Jones family. My mother, Janice, is a judge who jogs in June. Father, whose name is Justin, sells juke boxes and is a member of a jousting team. Uncle Jake is a jockey from Jersey, and Aunt Jane is a janitor in a jewelry store. The twins, Julie and Jesse, can do jigsaw puzzles in a jiffy.

And me? I'm going to say good-bye to my pet jellyfish and have a snack of juice and jiggly Jello before I leave on my long jet journey to a jump rope jamboree in Jamaica. Aren't you jealous?

GRAFFITI MURAL

PREPARATION:
On a large piece of mural paper, write several phrases which use one of the following words:

run	out	up
back	side	down
time	set	right

(See example.)

USE:
1. Fasten the mural to a wall or large bulletin board.
2. Talk with the students about words which have many uses. Ask them to add to the mural over a period of several days. Encourage them to use the dictionary and discuss possible uses with friends and family.
3. After a substantial number of ideas have been collected, work as a group, as individuals, or in small groups to combine several of the uses into paragraphs, stories, newspaper articles, or speeches.
4. Display the written pieces on or near the graffiti mural.
5. Try the activity again with a different word.

RUN

the run of the house
RUN OFF
run for office
RUN OUT OF MONEY
RUN INTO TROUBLE
run amok
run away
Run around in circles
run of the mill
runaround
RUN HOME to Mother
RUN THAT BY ME AGAIN
RUNNY NOSE
run in your stocking
RUN AGROUND
front runner
run the washer
run guns
HOME RUN
Run the gauntlet
run off with the money

GETTING IT ALL TOGETHER

Put these pictures in the right order and they will tell a story.

1. Determine the order of the pictures and number the pictures.
2. Then, for each one, write a sentence or two to describe the event. Vary the lengths and kinds of the sentences so that the story will be more interesting.
3. Finally, copy the story on clean paper, making any changes or corrections necessary to make an interesting, complete story.
4. Give the story a title and find a way to show off the finished product (illustrate it, frame it, publish it, etc.).

( )

( )

( )

( )

( )

( )

( )

( )

( )

( )

149

FOUND WRITING

This is a wonderful writing activity to save for a day when students don't feel like writing. It's done without pencil or pen!

PREPARATION:
- Gather magazines (to cut up), scissors, envelopes, construction paper, and glue.

USE:
1. Give each student one or two magazines, an envelope, and scissors. Tell the students to cut words and phrases from the magazines and put them in their envelopes. They should only cut out words they can read themselves. Allow 1/2 hour for this.
2. On the same day or another day, trade envelopes so that no student has his or her own.
3. Assign a writing activity to be done with the cut-out words. (This can vary according to the grade level and student abilities.) For example:

- a poem
- the inside of a valentine
- a warning
- an advertisement
- an invitation

- a piece of advice
- a ransom note
- a good idea
- three things never to say to an alligator

THE RULES ARE:
1. Students may not use a pen or pencil to write any words or letters.
2. They must write by pasting the words from their envelopes on construction paper. They may cut up the words and phrases to create new ones.

An APPLE A day fills YOU to the core

Love

a sweet little thing

vegetables?

favorite

something good.

The Mystery of the **BETTER BEGINNINGS**

1. Write on the board these two beginnings for a mystery story.

   The house on 14th Street was scary.
   The deserted, ramshackle house was dark and still as death.

2. Ask the students to discuss what makes the second sentence a better beginning.
3. Do the same with these beginnings:

   Michael heard some noises on the stairs.
   "Creeeaaaak," went the stairs behind him. Michael held his breath.

   and these:

   The three teenagers decided to go exploring in the attic.
   When the three teenagers decided to go exploring in the attic, none of them
      could have suspected what was about to happen.

4. If there's time, brainstorm for another good mystery beginning.

QUICK CHANGE AND REARRANGE

Writing is far more interesting to read if it contains a variety of sentences--some long, some short, some simple, some complex, some with the subject at the beginning, and some with the subject near the end.

Look at the example below. Do you see how **A** differs from **B**?

A The kids narrowly escaped from the waves which were crashing and pounding against the shore.

B Angry waves pounded the shore. The kids narrowly escaped their icy grasp.

Practice making different sentences so that you'll have some new ideas next time you write.

Rewrite each sentence. Sometimes you'll be given specific directions. Other times you'll be on your own to come up with a variation.

Cynthia had not ever considered that she might be a suspect.

Never _____

_____ .

"The lion, the alligator, the banker, and the popcorn man are all in this together, " concluded the detective.

(Put "concluded the detective" in the middle of the quote.)

_____

_____ .

The storm subsided, the wind stopped, the air became very still, and the town lay covered with a strange, damp quiet.

(Break this into several short sentences.)

_____

_____ .

Roberto reluctantly agreed to go waterskiing because the last time he tried it he never got up on the skis.

Because he never got up on the skis, _____

_____

_____ .

Michael turned the corner and gasped at what he saw on the sidewalk.

_____

_____ .

Three curious-looking strangers were lurking around the high school just before the big game.

_____

_____ .

The child stomped her little foot and shouted "NO!" as her mother's face grew redder.

_____

_____ .

The exhausted climbers were just about to the top of the mountain when they felt the rope beginning to give way.

(Make this a shorter sentence.) _____

_____ .

WORDS THAT MAKE A DIFFERENCE

A certain word in a certain place can make a lot of difference in the meaning or feeling of a sentence.

Write these sentences on the board. Talk with the students about how the effect is changed by replacing one word with another.

The sky was a dark gray.
The sky was an ominous gray.

"Why didn't you tell me?" she asked her sister.
"Why didn't you tell me?" she snarled at her sister.

Then, give the students a sentence or two (depending on the time), and ask them to replace the emphasized word with another which will make the sentence more clear, colorful, or interesting.

For example:

*Yesterday I noticed a man walking **slowly** around the block.*
*The ocean was a beautiful, deep **blue**.*
*No one had been in the **upstairs** bedroom for 25 years.*
*The monkeys **talked** among themselves noisily.*
*Until recently, I was sure the **old** lady next door was a witch.*
*Never before have I heard such **noise** in this classroom.*
*My sister **is very careful** to **hide** her diary every morning.*
*The fog horn sounded **sad** as it **cried** out over the harbor.*

The strange old woman opened the shade.

The eccentric matriarch stealthily raised the shade.

STUDY SKILLS

GIVE ME A "C"!

1. Cut large, white sheets of construction paper in half lengthwise.
2. Give each student one of these pieces of paper and instruct him or her to write a word beginning with *cha* in large letters. (They may consult a dictionary.)
3. Compare words and eliminate duplicates by asking several students to write new words.
4. With students holding on to their words, direct the group to alphabetize themselves.
5. Continue the game as long as desirable, using different beginning letters and letter groups.

   Note: The activity becomes even more challenging with difficult beginnings such as *con, inter, res, inco, uni,* etc.

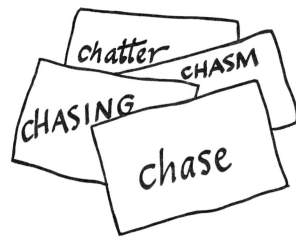

READ IT! DO IT! NAME IT!

WHAT AM I DOING WRONG?

How good are you at following directions? Test yourself and see what happens.

1. Cut along the dotted lines.

2. Fold forward along line 1.

3. Fold forward along line 2. (This will overlap.)

4. Write your name on section A.

5. Fold forward at line 3.

6. Fold backward at line 4.

7. Fold forward along line 5.

8. Stand up, hold the object high in the air as shown in the illustration, and let it drop to the ground.

9. What have you made? Give it a name!

Now try writing similar directions for a simple object of your own design. Trade with a friend to test your inventions!

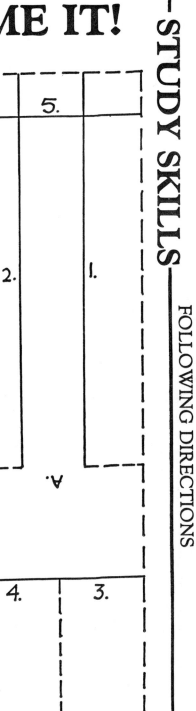

PAIR-A-GON OF INFORMATION

PREPARATION:
- Provide each student with two pieces of white paper, approximately 9 x 12 inches, one marker, and tape or pins.
- Choose a **content** reading assignment with much detailed information.

USE:
1. Ask the students to read the entire assignment.
2. Assign one section or paragraph to each student. ("Meaty" selections may be assigned to more than one student.)
3. The student uses one piece of paper to write a question based on the material in the assigned selection. The other paper is used to write the answer. (Writing should be in large, clear letters.)
4. Collect the QUESTIONS in one stack, the ANSWERS in another. Shuffle the stacks and give each student one question and one answer.
5. Have the students pin the questions on their backs and the answers on their chests. Each student proceeds to locate the person whose chest answers his or her question.
6. When called on, each "pair" stands before the class. Discuss the question and answer to help the class review the information read.

ONE, TWO, TREE!

PREPARATION:

- This activity was created as an alternative for those kids who find outlining with Roman numerals and letters a bit overwhelming. Providing more visual interest and motivation, this activity takes a bit of the drudgery out of organization.
- You will need a good social studies text and copies of the following work-study guide for each student.

USE:

1. Give the class a brief, well-organized reading assignment related to a country or region. Ask them to read it carefully.
2. Present the work-study guide labeled "Coun-tree".
3. Explain that this is another method of organizing the information they have just read, and ask them to work independently to do the first "branch" on geography. Share and discuss answers until you are satisfied that the students understand how to use the outline.
4. Ask the students to complete the outline on their own. (Later students may be given a second copy of the outline and assigned individual countries or regions.)
5. Use the "Personal-O-Tree" outline in a similar manner after students have read biographical books or articles.

"THE PERSONAL-O-TREE"

A work-study guide for organizing important BIOGRAPHICAL information

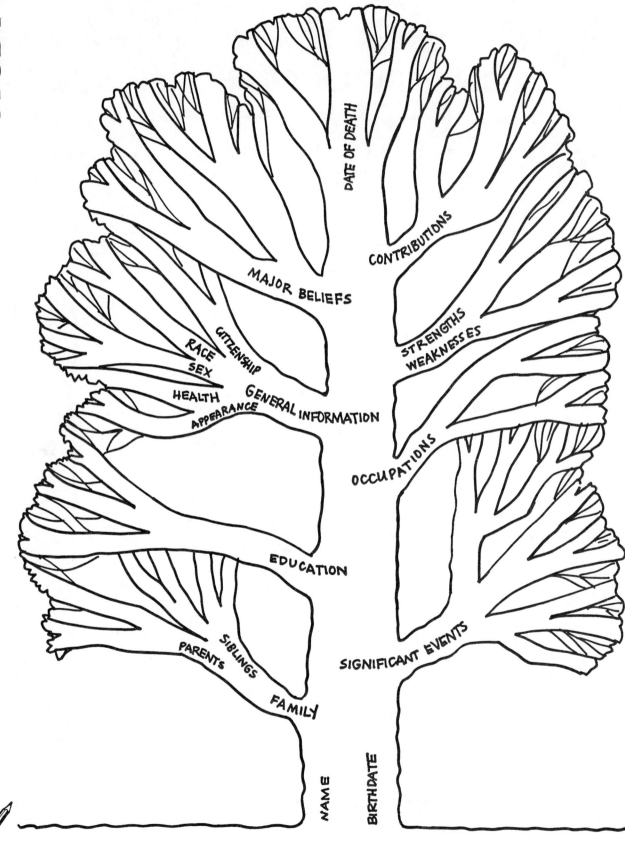

DATE OF DEATH

CONTRIBUTIONS

MAJOR BELIEFS

STRENGTHS

WEAKNESSES

CITIZENSHIP

RACE

SEX

HEALTH

GENERAL INFORMATION

APPEARANCE

OCCUPATIONS

EDUCATION

PARENTS

SIBLINGS

SIGNIFICANT EVENTS

FAMILY

NAME

BIRTHDATE

"THE COUN-TREE"

A work-study guide for organizing important information on the anatomy of a COUNTRY or a REGION

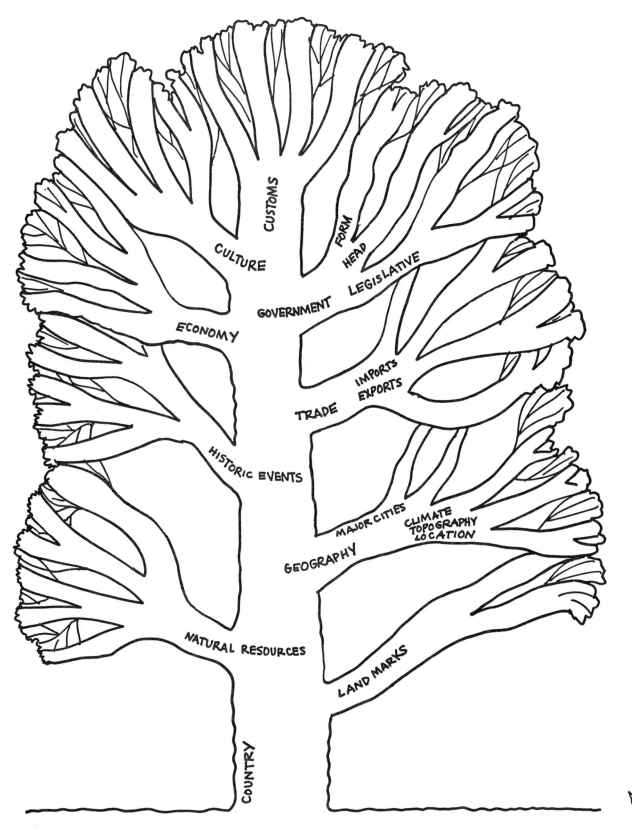

ERRAND EFFICIENCY QUOTIENT

. . . How's yours? As an adult, you will find one of your most needed skills will be that of getting necessary tasks accomplished quickly. That takes organization -- even for the most ordinary activities! See how efficiently you can organize these errands -- in TEN MINUTES or less!

You cannot leave the house until 3:00. Draw a line on the map to show your travel route. Then number the tasks in the order that you did them. Be on time . . . remember that the cat gets carsick . . . and don't let the ice cream melt!

TO DO:

___ Get cat to the vet
___ Leave pants at cleaners
___ Return books to library
___ Take cake to church bake sale
___ Leave film at photomat
___ Pick up Benji at ballpark by 5:00
___ Dental appointment at 3:30
___ Pick up fencing at hardware
___ Hamburger and ice cream for supper
___ Drop gift at Mrs. Bergen's
___ Mail package to Andy

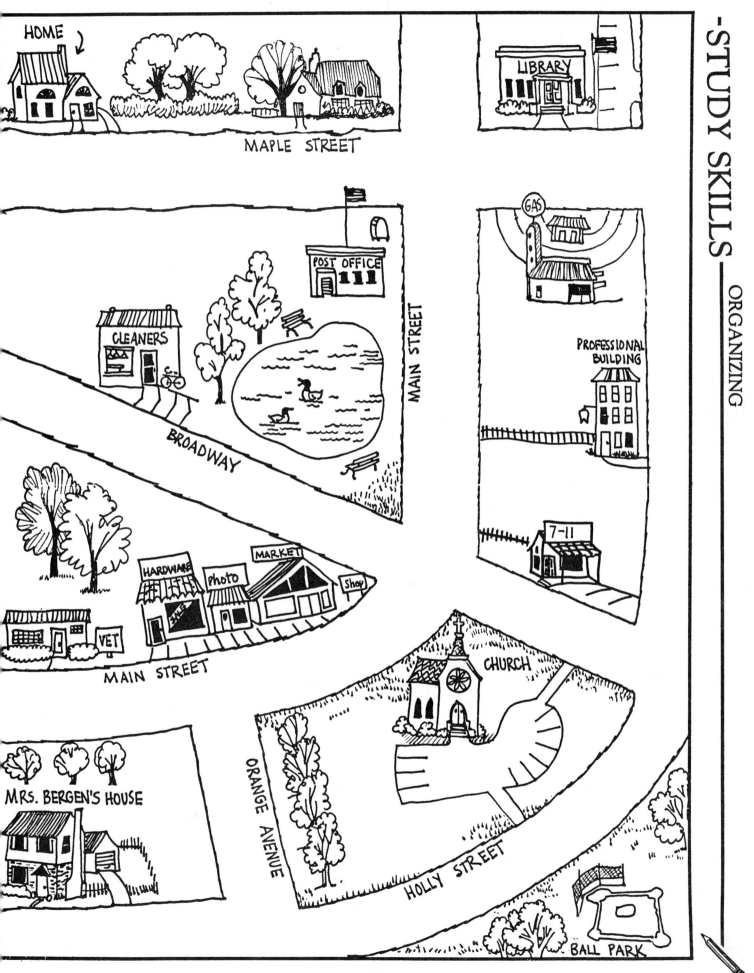

STUMP THE PANEL

PREPARATION:
- Choose a body of content to be read and "digested" by the entire class.
- All students need text, pencils and paper.

USE:
1. When it is time to read and study a science or social studies lesson, tell the class something like this: "Today we want to find out how heat travels. Only seven people will study the assignment. When they have become experts on heat, they will share what they have learned with the rest of us."

2. Choose seven people, give them the assigned pages, and tell them to find as much information about the subject as they can. They may take notes, gather props, and prepare themselves in any way to answer questions and explain what they have read.

3. Tell the rest of the class that their job is to stump the panel. They should prepare questions that they think the panel may not be able to answer, but the answers MUST appear in the assigned reading materials.

4. When everyone is ready, class members may take turns asking questions. The panel members may confer on answers. (This saves the poor reader from being the target of difficult questions.)

5. Score is kept by giving one point to the panel for correctly answered questions and one point to the questioners for each question not answered correctly. (The panel is not penalized for inability to answer questions for which information was not available in the assignment.)

You may be surprised how panel and class members equally benefit from this activity!

HAVE A HAPPY GRAPH

"Happy Birthday to you,....

Happy Birthday to you,....

Happy Birthday, dear Students!"

Number of Students	January	February	March	April	May	June	July	August	September	October	November	December

Title:

Use the back of this paper to write the name of each person in your class and the month of his or her birthday.

Use the information to create a vertical bar graph as shown above. Make it neat and colorful.

Add a title to the graph.

(Your graph should show how many birthdays fall in each month of the year.)

CHART SMART

PREPARATION:
- Divide the class into four or five equal committees.
- Provide poster paper, markers and rulers for making charts.

USE:
1. Assign one of the projects suggested below to each committee (or create similar projects suited to your students).
2. Committees should meet to plan how information may be gathered and to get needed permission.
3. Each committee should appoint one or more recorders to keep track of information.
4. When all pertinent information has been accumulated, each committee should create a chart summarizing what they have learned.

SUGGESTED PROJECTS:

The Eyes Have It!

PURPOSE:
- To discover the eye colors represented by boys and girls in each class or grade level in the school. Which is the most prevalent color for each group?

Breakfast Club

PURPOSE:
- To discover the most popular breakfast foods of two different grade groups by keeping track of what is actually eaten by each group for one week and then comparing the two groups.

Who's Here ?

PURPOSE:
- To discover average school attendance in each grade for a week. Which grade does the best each day and each week?

Go Guzzlers !

PURPOSE:
- To discover which grade guzzles the most milk or other beverage during one week.

Popularity Poll

PURPOSE:
- To discover the most popular color of a shirt or blouse as shown by wearing frequency during one week . . . by boys . . . by girls . . . or in one or more grade levels.

167

WEBSTER'S WORRY

PREPARATION:

- Students need to become familiar with dictionary format, understanding the form and purpose of each part of a dictionary entry.
- Students will need paper or cards of uniform size and shape on which to create their entries.

USE:

1. Each student must contribute one or more original nonsense words to a class dictionary. Each entry must include:

   a. original spelling
   b. phonetic spelling of the word, including stresses and syllabication
   c. the form class (part of speech)
   d. spelling of word with endings
   e. definitions
   f. illustrations, if possible

2. When all entries have been completed, make provisions for sharing the contributions orally. A committee may be appointed to alphabetize the entries and prepare the dictionary for "publication".

flib-ble (flib'l), v. [flibbling, flibbed], 1. to waddle. 2. to disagree in fun. n. [flibbles, flibbler], 3. One who waddles. 4. a short-billed bird with a tail that wobbles.

Skit-ter (ski'tĕr), v. [skittering, skittered] 1. to disperse quickly, spill. n. [skitters] 2. queasy feeling in the stomach. 3. Small skateboard with wheels.

DEFINE IT OR FAKE IT!

PREPARATION:
- Students need dictionaries.
- Panel members need paper and pencil.
- The teacher needs a list of words unfamiliar to most students.

USE:
1. Choose a "team" of about six people to form a panel of "definition detectives". Arrange a place for them to sit in front of the room.

2. Write a word on the board which is not known by any of the students (i.e., declivity, intrepid, onyx). For best learning results, choose words which you'd like the students to learn.

3. All students on the panel pretend to check the dictionary, but only one panel member (predetermined by the panel for each turn) actually looks up the word and copies its definition. The other five write plausible definitions.

4. The teacher (or each student) then reads the definitions, and the remaining class members vote for the "definition" they think is correct.

5. Then, all class members may consult their dictionaries and discuss the real meaning.

6. Repeat the same procedure with other words and with different panels.

FIND THE COMMON DENOMINATOR

PREPARATION:
- Compile a list of word pairs which have similar meanings.
- Prepare a large chart containing questions that compare the words. Post this chart in a corner or learning center containing several dictionaries.

USE:
1. Ask students to visit the center and use the dictionary to answer the questions.
2. Each participant must add a question to the list, using words that are likely to stump classmates.
3. When all students have visited the center, everyone must visit again to answer the questions added since their first visit.
4. When everyone has had a chance to become familiar with the word pairs, use the assembled list of questions as a fun five-minute filler!

SAMPLE QUESTIONS:

a. *How is a skiff like a lugger?*

b. *What do fuchsia and mignonette have in common?*

c. *How is a flume like a gorge?*

d. *What is the same about a coracle and a raft?*

e. *How is a cormorant like an albatross?*

f. *Where would you find a brougham and a buggy?*

g. *How is a merino like a ewe?*

h. *Where would you find a medulla and a cerebrum?*

170

MISSING LINKS

You've heard of the "missing link", but you probably never expected to find it hidden in the pages of a reference book!

Each name listed below is really a combination of two names.
To find the "missing link", try to discover the name that goes between the two names and fits with both.

EXAMPLE: Babe Saint Denis
The missing link is RUTH.
Babe Ruth and Ruth Saint Denis.

Since many names will not be familiar to you, you will need to look up the names in an encyclopedia or other reference book containing names. If there is more than one entry for a last name, experiment by inserting different first names.

TRY THESE!

1. William O. MacArthur _____ _____

2. Benjamin Roosevelt _____ _____

3. Sault Ste. Antoinette _____ _____

4. Sir Walter Carpenter _____ _____

5. Sinclair Carroll _____ _____

6. Patrick Ford _____ _____

7. Prince de Gaulle _____ _____

8. O. Kissinger _____ _____

9. Booker T. Irving _____ _____

10. Anne Lloyd Wright _____ _____

*   See answers on page 240.

Create some missing links of your own on the back of this page!

171

HEADLINE HEROES

Under which headline would you most likely find a story mentioning each of the following names? Enter the corresponding letter of the headline by each name. (Your encyclopedia will be a great help!)

—— Gloria Steinhem

—— Abby Hoffman

—— Billy Graham

—— Chris Evert

—— Jane Fonda

—— Richard M. Nixon

—— O.J. Simpson

—— Neil Armstrong

—— The Beatles

—— Patty Hearst

—— Adolf Hitler

—— Susan B. Anthony

* See page 240 for answers.

A. WATERGATE, A Bad Memory

B. STAR SPEAKS OUT ON VIETNAM

C. NEWSPAPER HEIRESS KIDNAPPED!

D. HE WANTS TO "RULE THE WORLD"

E. Woman leads "RIGHT TO VOTE" March

F. RUNNING HALFBACK TAKES THE HEISMAN!!

G. FAMOUS "CHICAGO SEVEN" STRIKES AGAIN!

H. Another First For Mankind!!!

I. Which Whirligig Whiz Won Wimbledon?

J. Women's Rights Conference Begins Monday

K. Quartet ROCKS western World.

L. Evangelical Crusade Begins Today

EXTRA! EXTRA!!

HISTORIC MOMENTS MYSTERY

Use the **"clue"** words, your **encyclopedia** and other **reference books** to pinpoint the historic event that took place and the year.

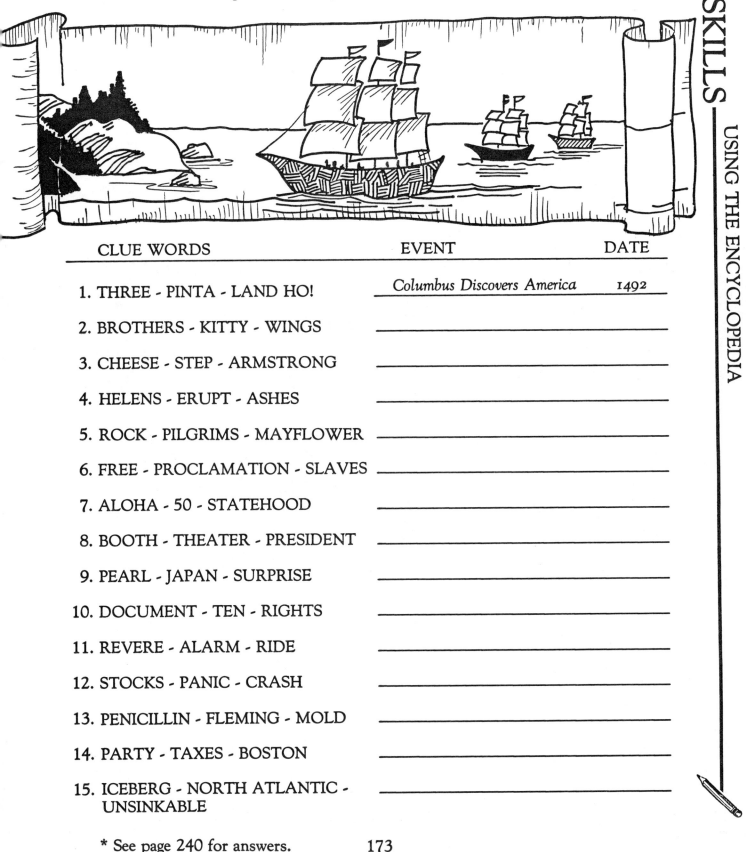

CLUE WORDS	EVENT	DATE
1. THREE - PINTA - LAND HO!	*Columbus Discovers America*	*1492*
2. BROTHERS - KITTY - WINGS		
3. CHEESE - STEP - ARMSTRONG		
4. HELENS - ERUPT - ASHES		
5. ROCK - PILGRIMS - MAYFLOWER		
6. FREE - PROCLAMATION - SLAVES		
7. ALOHA - 50 - STATEHOOD		
8. BOOTH - THEATER - PRESIDENT		
9. PEARL - JAPAN - SURPRISE		
10. DOCUMENT - TEN - RIGHTS		
11. REVERE - ALARM - RIDE		
12. STOCKS - PANIC - CRASH		
13. PENICILLIN - FLEMING - MOLD		
14. PARTY - TAXES - BOSTON		
15. ICEBERG - NORTH ATLANTIC - UNSINKABLE		

* See page 240 for answers.

HERE'S JOHNNY!

Below are surnames of famous men whose first names are all the same.
Match each of the names with an object that person might logically possess. Check the encyclopedia for difficult matches!

_____ Phillip Sousa

_____ Alden

_____ Adams

_____ Chapman

_____ Dillinger

_____ Bench

_____ McEnroe

INDEX IN DEPTH

PREPARATION:
- Provide a quiet corner or learning center containing several kinds of indexes:

Sears' catalog	Sunday paper
telephone book	Readers' Guide to
(with Yellow Pages)	Periodicals
index volume to encyclopedia	school directory

- In the center, place a list of questions which can be answered by using the indexes. (See examples below.)

USE:
1. Each student who visits the center may choose ten questions to answer, or the teacher may suggest certain questions which fit the needs and abilities of a student.
2. When the chosen or assigned questions have been answered, the student then adds at least two original questions.
3. After all students have had an opportunity to visit the center, spot-check skill and understanding by doing a five-minute drill (without papers) to see if the students know which index to utilize for each question.

SAMPLE QUESTIONS:

Name three places you may call to get an estimate for repairing your roof.

Write the price of Sears' best automatic ice cream maker.

Name three movies now showing in downtown theaters.

Who are the room mothers for Miss Vogetl's class in the middle school?

Name two magazine articles on the population explosion.

List three places in the encyclopedia where information can be found related to the Statue of Liberty.

HOW FAR IS FAR EAST?

If you needed to know the answers to the following questions, what **key words** would you look up . . . and where would you look for them? In the encyclopedia? Almanac? Dictionary? Thesaurus? Atlas?

Write your **key words** and **possible sources** (there is often more than one) in the spaces provided.

Then choose five questions to which you do not already know the answer. Write the answers to those questions with their corresponding numbers on the spaces provided.

		KEY WORDS	POSSIBLE REFERENCES
1.	How far from home is the Far East?	*Eastern Hemisphere* *Far East* *China, Japan*	*World Atlas,* *Encyclopedia* *Dictionary*
2.	Who won the women's figure skating event in the 1976 Olympic Games?		
3.	Who would use a micrometer caliper?		
4.	Where would one find a dingo?		
5.	Do groundhogs hibernate?		
6.	How many planets are there in the solar system?		
7.	How many different meanings are there for the word battery?		
8.	What is Charlie Brown's age?		
9.	How large was the world's greatest pumpkin?		
10.	What is the object pictured beside **A**?		

11. What main holidays are celebrated in China? _____

12. What is the best way to carve a roast? _____

13. What ten words are synonyms for delightful? _____

14. Which country in Europe has the highest elevation? _____

15. What is the number for the Child Abuse Hotline? _____

16. Who is the tallest man on record? _____

17. How many U.S. cities have names that begin with LOVE? _____

18. Which is larger in area . . . Africa or South America? _____

19. Name a few of Italy's most famous artists. _____

20. What kind of architecture is shown beside **B**? _____

A.  B.

. . . AND HERE ARE THE BIG FIVE!

\# —— _____

\# —— _____

\# —— _____

\# —— _____

\# —— _____

TRAVELERS ABROAD

PREPARATION:
- Provide each student with a copy of the next page.
- Be sure that pens, crayons, colored markers and reference materials are readily available.

USE:
1. Ask the students to pretend that they are on a holiday trip to one of the following cities. (They should choose one they have not visited before.)

London	Venice	Rome	Lisbon
Cairo	Tokyo	Paris	Berne
Bonn	Helsinki	Peking	Amsterdam
Sydney	Dublin	Moscow	Mexico City
West Berlin	Quito	Brussels	Jerusalem
Stockholm	Singapore	Beirut	Rio de Janeiro
Honolulu	Vienna	Athens	Panama City

2. Reference materials should be available so that students may become acquainted with their chosen cities.
3. It is now an "afternoon break" on an exhaustive city tour, and they are writing post cards to friends at home.
4. Ask them to use the front of the "post card" to create a picture that shows one of their favorite attractions or discoveries in the city, and to use the back to write a note telling as much as possible about the place they are visiting. They should address the card to a friend.
5. Supply a center or display area where the cards may be shared to provide a glimpse of many major world cities.

HOW TO BE A HERO

PREPARATION:

- Provide each student with a copy of the HOW TO BE A HERO research guide (next page).
- Be sure students have access to appropriate reference materials.
- Prepare the following list of acknowledged heroes/heroines.

Gen. Douglas MacArthur
Paul Bunyan
Will Rogers
Franklin D. Roosevelt
Althea Gibson
Mary Lou Retton
Jonas Salk
Harriet Tubman
Abraham Lincoln
Harry Houdini
Superman

Dorothy Hamill
Sir Lancelot
Neil Armstrong
Genghis Khan
Joan of Arc
Babe Ruth
Martin Luther King
John F. Kennedy
Johnny Appleseed
Golda Meir

USE:

1. Discuss the definition of a hero/heroine. How do people become heroes/heroines? Ask the students to consider whether there are common personal traits and characteristics or circumstances shared by most people in this category.
2. Ask each student to choose from the list at least three names to research and compare, using the format of the research guide.
3. Provide time for sharing results of the project in small groups. Create a center or display area where notes and illustrative material might be collected and remain as reference material for an appropriate time.
4. When the project is complete, consider again, as a class, the role of common characteristics and circumstances in the creation of heroes/heroines.

HOW TO BE A HERO...A RESEARCH GUIDE

What makes a hero or heroine? What kind of "stuff" does it take? Is there a group of characteristics common to most people who are admired by the world? A good way to answer this question is to study the lives of some acknowledged heroes or heroines and compare the similarities.

Use the space below to take some brief research notes about three famous people.

NAME			
SEX / RACE			
PHYSICAL APPEARANCE			
PARENTS			
SIBLINGS			
FRIENDS			
HEALTH			
EDUCATION			
RELIGION			
MAIN OCCUPATION			
LEADERSHIP QUALITIES			
PERSONAL SENSITIVITY			
PERSONAL INTERESTS			
MEMORABLE ACTS/ CONTRIBUTIONS			
WEAKNESSES			
CONCERN FOR HUMANITY			
AGE BECAME KNOWN			

Locate a picture or drawing of each of the above persons or create a related drawing or object to share with the class.

BEST BET!

PREPARATION:
- Write this list of reference materials on the chalkboard:

  Encyclopedia   Almanac
  Dictionary   World Atlas
  Thesaurus   Guiness Book of Records
  Rhyming Dictionary   Readers' Guide

- Prepare five or six questions similar to the ones below, appropriate for the skill and interest levels of the students.

  ### SAMPLE QUESTIONS:
  How do rabbits protect themselves?
  *What word meaning **fast** rhymes with **drift**?*
  How far is it from New York City to Dallas, Texas?
  What happened on this day 100 years ago?
  Who is the tallest person in the world?
  *Name ten synonyms for the word **happy**.*
  Would you order a hackie at a restaurant?

USE:
1. Begin by presenting questions such as these. Ask students to identify the reference source that would provide the most efficient answer.
2. The student who answers makes up the next question and calls on someone who has not had a turn.
3. Continue as long as time permits or until all have had a turn.

TRAVEL LOGIC

Mr. Tuttle, Mrs. Spain, and Miss Pillsbury took holiday trips from Chicago to foreign countries. One went to Switzerland, one went to Zaire, and one went to Australia.

Use the following clues to figure out who went where.

1. Mrs. Spain did not go to Switzerland.
2. Mr. Tuttle did not go to Australia.
3. Miss Pillsbury did not go to Zaire.
4. Mr. Tuttle did not go to Zaire.
5. Miss Pillsbury went to the most southern country.

Country

Mr. Tuttle   _____
Mrs. Spain   _____
Miss Pillsbury   _____

"YOU MUST RESPOND IMMEDIATELY!"

"I'M SO EXCITED, I COULD BURST!"

"Oh, YOU ARE JUST TOO CUTE!"

ROCKET CAT

APTLY ADVERBIAL

Use your **thesaurus** to locate at least four different **adverbs**, any one of which would make a terrific ending to each sentence.

Write the four adverbs in the second blank below each sentence. Then choose the very **best** one to complete the sentence.

"You must respond immediately!" barked Sgt. Grouss

_____ .

_____

"Nyeah, nyeah, I got more than you did," teased Ryan

_____ .

_____

"Why, I don't know . . . I really can't remember," the old man stammered _____ .

_____

"I'm so excited, I could burst!" Georgette squealed

_____ .

_____

"I prefer my doughnuts *without* apostrophes!" Miss Pruitt snipped _____ .

_____

"Columbus, you have discovered enough!" quipped Elizabeth

_____ .

_____

"Yuk, this soup has curdled!" the princess choked _____

_____ .

_____

"Oh, you are just too cute!" squealed the teeny-bopper

_____ .

_____

184

ALL IN THE FAMILY

PREPARATION:

- Each student needs a thesaurus, colored construction paper, scissors, and pen or pencil.

USE:

1. Ask each student to cut a large house shape from construction paper.
2. As they are doing so, assign each student one of the following categories:

children	curiosity	color	money
dance	time	measurement	law
food	skiing	love	climate
rocks	secrets	space	books
mystery	the sea	mountains	winter
baseball	distress	anger	ice
summer	fashion	fishing	heart
mischief	terrorism	joy	houses
war	comedy	lips	motion
politics	success	earth	education
fire	family	government	celebration

3. Each student uses the thesaurus to fill the house with as many related words as possible. (Students are not limited to synonyms!)
4. Provide a place where the word-family homes may be displayed. The houses may then be used as bases for writing assignments or further word study.

185

A NOVEL BLUEPRINT

A NOVEL BY MANFRED

A MILLION SELLER!

Pretend you are committed to a publisher to create the most fascinating textbook ever written on your favorite subject.

Study the covers, title pages, forewords and tables of contents of as many textbooks as possible to see how they look and to understand what kinds of information they supply.

Now . . . make a plan to present the most visually exciting and stimulating text that your publisher has ever seen. Not wanting to see the finished product yet, the publisher wants only these parts:

Cover   **Title Page**   **Foreword**   **Table of Contents**

If your plan is really great, you might get a chance to present it to a real publisher some day. Go to it!

TABLE ABLE

PREPARATION:
- Choose a text which has an extensive table of contents. Be sure each student has a copy.

USE:
1. Ask the students to locate the table of contents in the text you have chosen. Give them a minute or two to skim the contents and become familiar with its organization.
2. Divide the class into four equal teams. Number the members of each team.
3. Ask a question whose answer can be found by locating a section in the table of contents and turning to those pages to read.

CONTENTS

UNIT I EARTH
The Solar System........4
Maps and Globes........12
Earth's Climate........17
UNIT II MOUNTAIN RANGES
European Alps.........19
The Andes.........26
Rockies.........46
UNIT III DESERT REGIONS
Gobi Desert.........53
Sahara Desert.........62
Death Valley.........70
UNIT IV - OCEANS
Pacific.........82

For Example:

a. How does the book define a desert?
b. What tribe lives on the Veldt plains?
c. What is an important product of America's western coast?
d. What large lake is found in the Andes Mountains?
e. Based on the climate only, where in the U.S. would you most like to live?

4. All students search for the answers. When most are ready, call a number (six, for example). Team member six from each team goes to the board to write the answer.

The first team with a correctly written answer wins a point.

I STARTED DATING IN JANUARY!

DATING SERVICE, ANYONE?

PREPARATION:
- Supply a large calendar for the current year (preferably one containing extra information -- holidays, moon information, etc.).
- Provide a list of questions requiring careful reading of the dates and information on the calendar.

USE:
1. Individuals may choose 12 questions to answer. (A prepared answer sheet will allow them to correct their own papers.)
2. Each student may be asked to add a question to the list.

SAMPLE QUESTIONS:

If today is June 17 and I am sailing to India on August 3, how many days must I wait?

Is this a leap year?

Is there a month that begins on Wednesday? Is it true that a month that begins on Wednesday will never end on Thursday?

Seven weeks from today the date will be _____ .

My dog goes wild under a full moon. What days in August should I keep him in the house?

It's April 25. If I have to wait more than nine weeks for the first day of summer, I will pull my hair out! Will I go bald?

I have a package for my sweetheart. It takes at least 13 days for mail to get from my house to hers. What is the last day I can mail it and be sure it gets there for Valentine's Day?

Twelve weeks, six days before Halloween is _____ .
Why not plan your pumpkin-face carving now?

BORDER PUZZLE

Each set of "squiggly" lines below represents segments of the borders between three or more states. Use your atlas to identify each group of states and label them correctly.

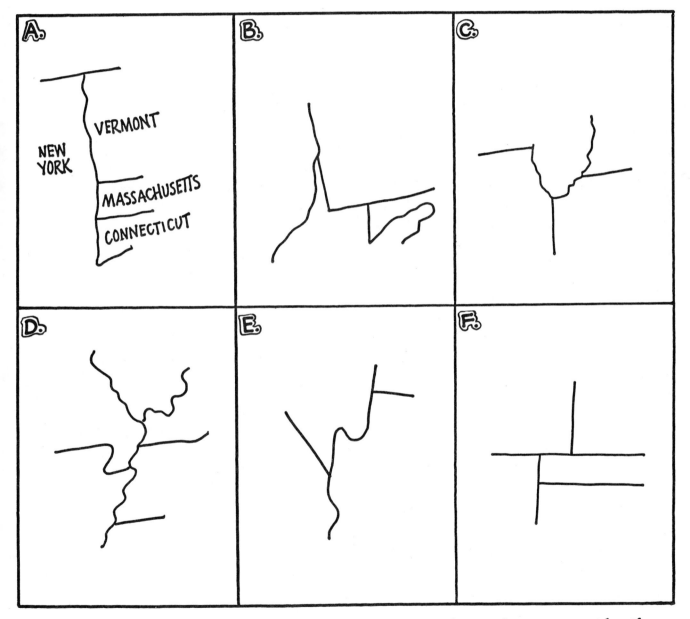

Create some additional border puzzlers of your own. See if your classmates can identify them.

For answers, see page 240.

189

TRAVEL, INC.

PREPARATION:
- Provide each student with a copy of the WORLD MAP on the next page.
- Prepare a box of 5 x 7 inch "trip" cards. Each card lists a departure and destination point.

USE:
1. Ask each student to draw a "trip" card. The task is to plan a trip between the two points.
2. The following information should be recorded on the back of the card:

   - location of two points by latitude & longitude

   - means of travel

   - direction of travel

   - approximate distance to be traveled

   - name of at least three other geographical locations along the route of travel

   - estimated time trip will take

3. Students must also trace the travel route on the world map, marking the departure, destination and three intermediate locations.

BANGKOK, THAILAND TO ANCHORAGE, ALASKA

PHOENIX, AZ. TO MOSCOW, U.S.S.R.

TOKYO, JAPAN TO MIAMI, FLORIDA

LONDON, ENGLAND TO HONOLULU, HAWAII

"TRIP" Cards

Note: Samples of real tour plans, plane, train and boat schedules, cruise listings, brochures, and pictures obtained from travel agencies or magazines will make the plans more detailed and fun.

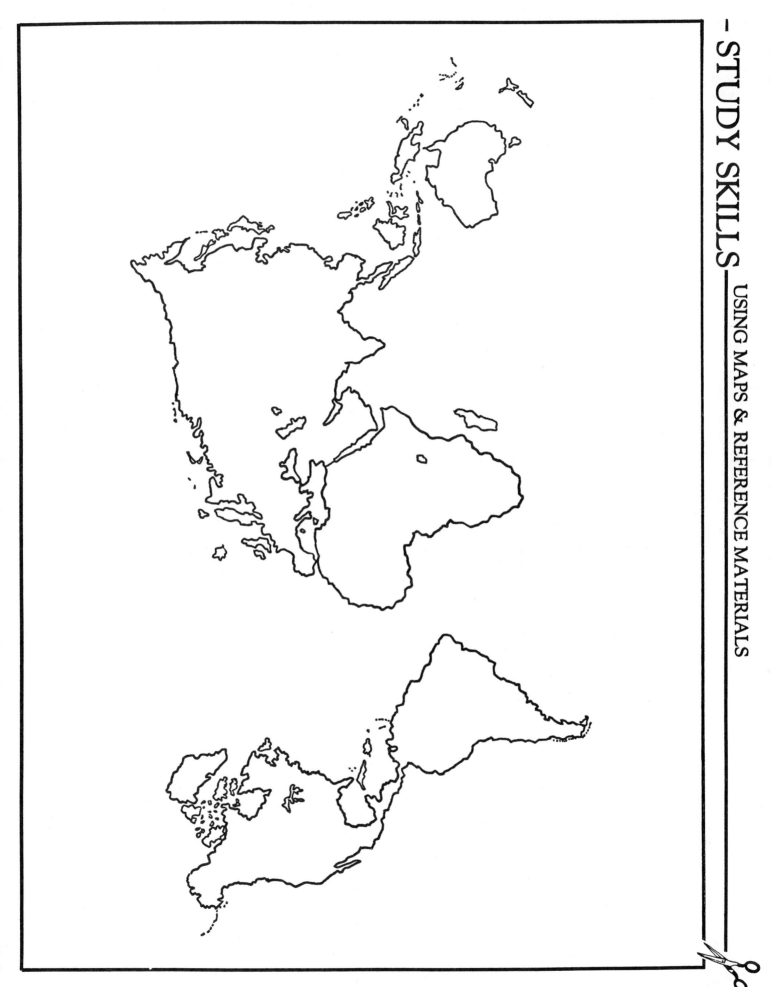

MAPMAKER, MAPMAKER, MAKE ME A MAP

PREPARATION:
- Reproduce copies of the next page for students.
- Provide directions such as the examples below.

USE:

1. Ask students to follow written directions such as these to create simple maps using original symbols and a key.

   - Label the directions on the map.

   - Label the east-west street MAIN Street.

   - Label the easternmost north-south road EASTERN Ave.

   - Label the westernmost north-south road AXLE Ave.

   - Label the central north-south road EDENS Ave.

   - Place a church on the southwest corner of MAIN and AXLE.

   - Give a name to the bike path that follows EASTERN Ave.

   - Label the road that runs from southwest to northeast EISENHOWER Parkway.

   - Draw a forest preserve along the eastern edge of AXLE, north of the EISENHOWER Parkway.

   - Draw a school on the southwest corner of EASTERN and MAIN.

   - Place a shopping plaza north of MAIN and just east of EDENS.

   - Create a community of homes south of MAIN between EDENS and AXLE.

   - Put a park east of EDENS and north of the EISENHOWER Parkway.

   - Draw a fire station on the northwest corner of MAIN and EDENS.

   - Put a stadium across from the school on EASTERN, and a swimming pool east of EASTERN and south of the EISENHOWER Parkway.

   - Draw a key for your map which explains all symbols.

2. Compare and discuss completed maps. (A self-checking key will help.) Students may wish to create other instructions for additions to their maps.

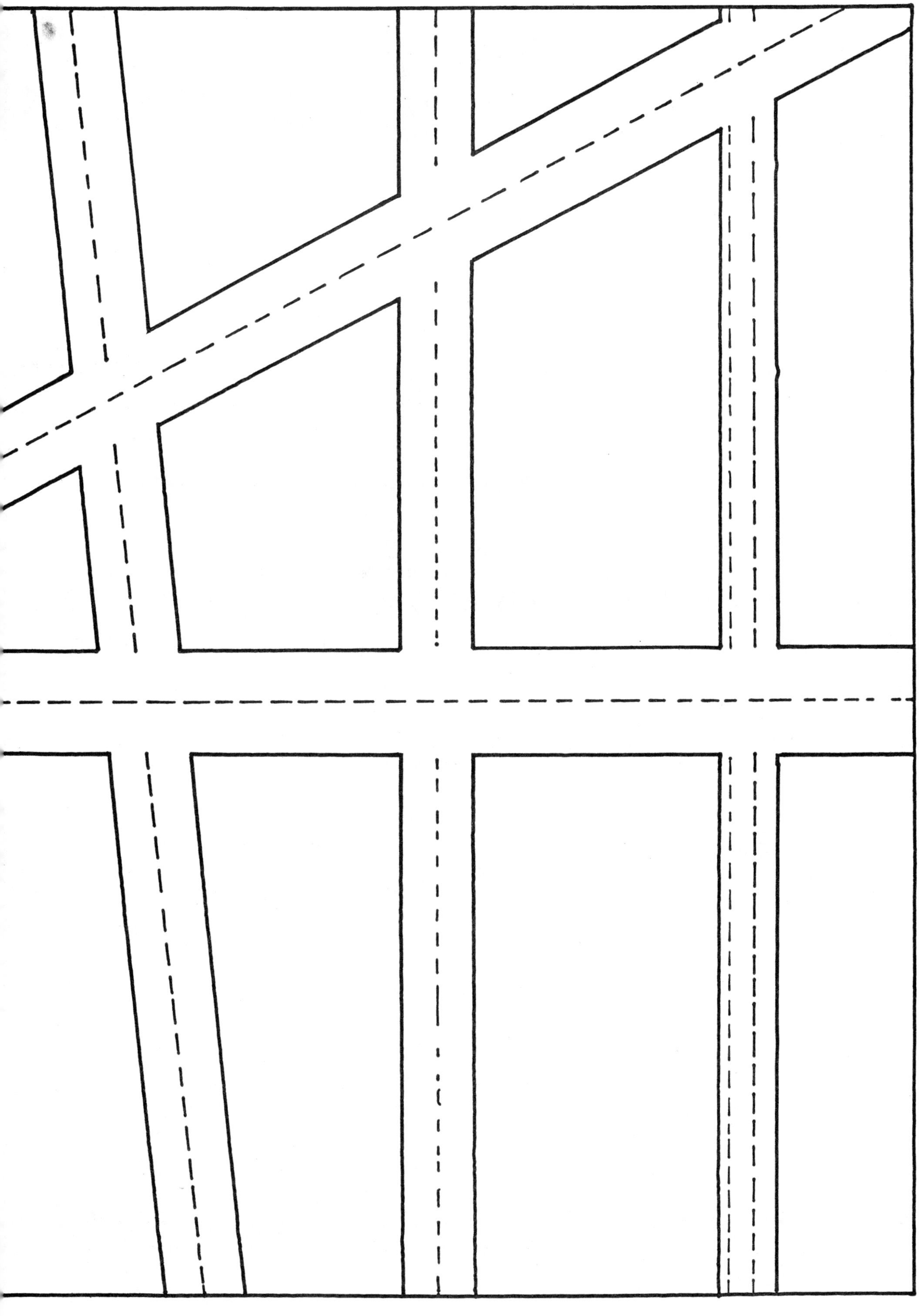

INVITATION TO ELLEFONT

The Legendary Kingdom of Ellefont

On the accompanying page are four maps of the fictitious country of ELLEFONT. Each map tells something different about the country.

POLITICAL MAP - shows the divisions of the country into states, provinces, counties, etc.

POPULATION MAP - shows the distribution of people in the country

TOPOGRAPHICAL MAP - shows what the land is like

PRECIPITATION MAP - shows comparative amounts of snow & rain for regions of the country

Study each map carefully. Below, write at least two observations related to the purpose of each map.

Political map: 1. _____

2. _____

Population Map: 1. _____

2. _____

Topographical Map: 1. _____

2. _____

Precipitation Map: 1. _____

2. _____

On another paper, draw a map of a country you have created. Choose one of the kinds of maps used here to show something specific about your country. Be sure to include a key! Give your country an interesting name.

Ellefont

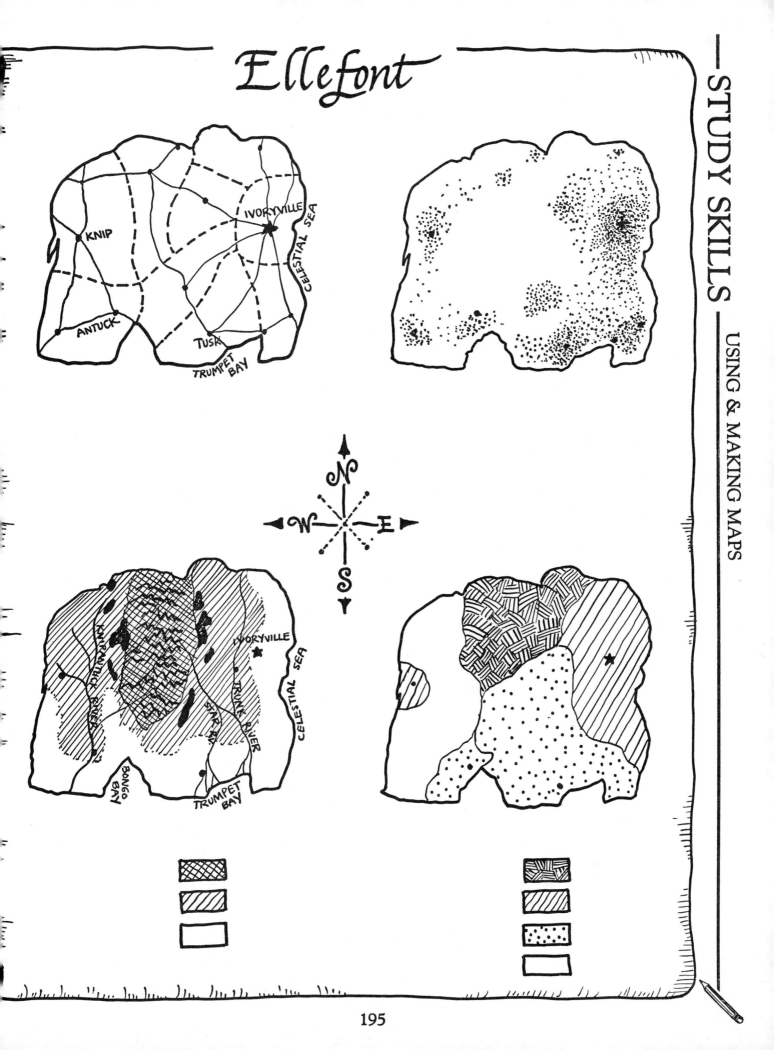

SHAPE OF A NATION

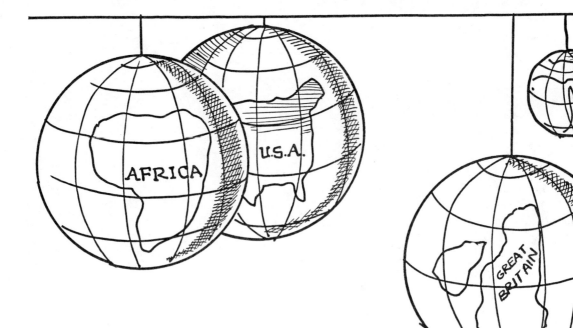

PREPARATION:
- Provide a large, light blue or white construction-paper circle for each student.
- Make available colored paper scraps, markers, pens, pencils, paste and string.

USE:
1. Ask each student to choose a different world nation.
2. Have each student create an outline map of that area of the world on the circle provided. (This will be referred to as each student's globe.)
3. To highlight the particular nation, each student should cut out its shape from brightly colored construction paper and place it in the proper place on his or her globe.
4. Tell students to write the name of the nation on the back of the globe and to use the string to hang it in an appointed display area.
5. Use the hanging globes to help students become familiar with the geographical locations and topographical "shapes" of the nations.

   Note: The teacher may create fun, five-minute activities related to the globes.

GLOBAL SCHOLARS

PREPARATION:
- Provide a corner where pairs of students may work with globes.
- Supply string, rulers, pencils, two globes, and a short list of questions which can be answered by reading information from the globes.

USE:
1. Ask each student to select a partner. The pair works together to answer the questions presented in the center, then creates three additional questions to be answered by the next pair to visit the center. (Of course, they must be sure to have the correct answers to their own questions and be ready to defend them with hard evidence!)
2. Each student pair answers the teacher's questions PLUS the one set created by the students preceding them in the center. When they have finished, the pair takes their answers to the preceding pair for checking.
3. Much discussion and "teaching" may take place. Hopefully, much learning will accompany the process!

What is the latitude of Madrid, Spain?

About how far is it from Liberia to Rhodesia?

What country includes this location?

60° N latitude
80° E longitude

What is the shortest route from Vancouver, Canada, to New Delhi, India?

IF TIME IS SO SHORT, WHY ARE TIME LINES SO LONG?

PREPARATION:
- Provide reference books for checking dates of special world events, a piece of butcher or mural paper several yards long, and markers.
- Provide a copy of the next page for each student.

USE:
1. Ask the students to employ reference materials to find the birth or anniversary dates associated with the events listed.
2. Assign to a small group of students the task of creating an outline format for a time line with space to include all the dates on the list. They should mark the time line in 10 - 20 year equal spaces as a guide for the necessary entries.
3. Assign each student an event to enter on the time line. After each student has added an entry, review the entire time line to help the students develop a feel for the span of time between historic events.
4. Students may illustrate the edges of the time line mural to add interest. The mural may be displayed for an appropriate period of time.

IF TIME IS SO SHORT, WHY ARE TIME LINES SO LONG?

Use reference materials to locate the dates on which these events took place.

Beethoven's birth _____

Emancipation Proclamation signed _____

Ratification of U.S. Constitution _____

Attack on Pearl Harbor Day _____

Monroe Doctrine signed _____

First American in space _____

Paul Revere's ride _____

End of World War II _____

Elizabeth II crowned queen _____

First pilgrims land at Plymouth _____

President Washington's inauguration _____

Noah Webster's birth _____

Richard M. Nixon resigned _____

Discovery of gold in California _____

Boston Tea Party _____

J.F. Kennedy assassinated _____

President Lincoln's inauguration _____

Man's first walk on moon _____

William Shakespeare's birth _____

* See page 240 for answers.

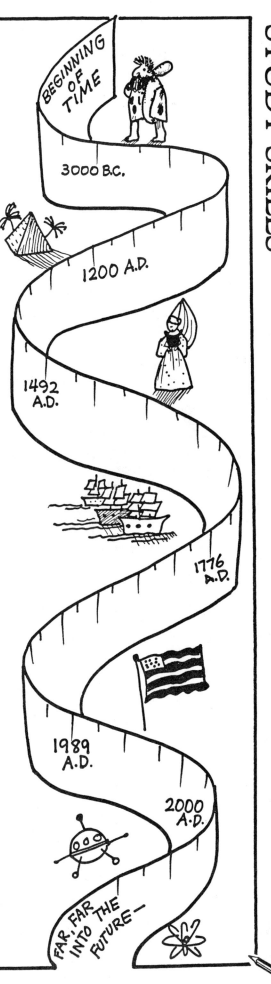

WHERE IT'S ALWAYS CHRISTMAS

Did you know . . . it's always Chirstmas in Florida . . . and if you follow the yellow brick road, you're likely to end up in Kentucky?

Use a road atlas to locate these unusual U.S. towns. Determine the nearest large city to each and look up the Zip codes of the large cities in a Zip code directory. Record the state abbreviations, nearest large cities, and Zip codes below.

State abbrev.   Nearest Large City   Zip code

CHRISTMAS, FLORIDA
SANTA CLAUS, INDIANA
GOODNIGHT, TEXAS
STANDING GROUND, KENTUCKY
DIFFICULT, TENNESSEE
CUCKOO, VIRGINIA
PLUTO, WEST VIRGINIA
SLAP OUT, ILLINOIS
BIG CHIEF, CALIFORNIA
PULLTIGHT, ALABAMA
BEAVER, LOUISIANA
WOODSTOCK, VERMONT
SLIPPERY ROCK, PENNSYLVANIA
WHYNOT, MISSISSIPPI

NEXT STOP—
PLUTO,
WEST VIRGINIA!

* See page 240 for answers.

VOCABULARY SKILLS CHECKLIST

Student's Name	Grade	Date	Teacher's Name

SKILLS   NOTES

___ Identifying synonyms
___ Identifying, using, and distinguishing between antonyms
___ Identifying, using,and distinguishing between homophones
___ Identifying and using prefixes
___ Identifying and using suffixes
___ Identifying and using root words
___ Understanding meanings of common prefixes and suffixes
___ Understanding meanings of common root words
___ Identifying multiple meanings of words
___ Understanding differences in connotation
___ Determining a word's meaning from its context
___ Finding and understanding word origins
___ Developing an appreciation for words
___ Developing a sensitivity to word sounds and rhythms
___ Classifying words according to use, meaning, and other purposes
___ Identifying and using puns
___ Identifying and using idioms
___ Identifying and using the following figures of speech:
    ___ *onomatopoeia*   ___ *simile*
    ___ *metaphor*   ___ *personification*
    ___ *hyperbole*   ___ *alliteration*
___ Choosing words for a specific purpose
___ Discriminating between words with similar sounds or spellings
___ Discriminating between words with similar meanings
___ Learning new words to expand the vocabulary
___ Expanding the use of words already known

202

GRAMMAR & USAGE SKILLS CHECKLIST

| Student's Name | Grade | Date | Teacher's Name |

SKILLS   ## NOTES

___ Understanding and using rules of capitalization
___ Understanding and using the following punctuation
marks: colon, comma, period, exclamation point,
question mark, parentheses, hyphen, semicolon,
apostrophe, underlining
___ Using and writing contractions properly
___ Understanding and writing abbreviations
___ Identifying and using a variety of sentence types:

    ___ *Declarative*   ___ *Simple*
    ___ *Interrogative*   ___ *Compound*
    ___ *Imperative*   ___ *Complex*

___ Identifying the following parts of speech:

    ___ *Subjects and predicates*
    ___ *Simple and complete subjects and predicates*
    ___ *Compound subjects and predicates*
    ___ *Direct and indirect objects*
    ___ *Singular and plural nouns*
    ___ *Common and proper nouns*
    ___ *Possessive nouns*
    ___ *Action verbs*
    ___ *Helping verbs*
    ___ *Linking verbs*
    ___ *Regular and irregular verbs*
    ___ *Transitive and intransitive verbs*
    ___ *Present, past, and future tenses of verbs*
    ___ *Subjective pronouns*
    ___ *Objective pronouns*
    ___ *Possessive pronouns*
    ___ *Demonstrative pronouns*
    ___ *Indefinite pronouns*
    ___ *Reflexive pronouns*
    ___ *Interrogative pronouns*
    ___ *Relative pronouns*
___ Understanding and using rules of phonetic
spelling

" ADJECTIVE ADVERB
, VERB NOUN
. ! ; PRONOUN "

READING SKILLS CHECKLIST

_____   _____   _____   _____
Student's Name   Grade   Date   Teacher's Name

SKILLS   NOTES

___ Reading for a specific purpose
___ Reading for details
___ Recalling information
___ Locating information quickly
___ Identifying author's purpose
___ Identifying author's bias
___ Comparing points of view
___ Identifying character traits
___ Identifying mood
___ Identifying style
___ Comparing styles
___ Determining the main idea
___ Identifying supporting details
___ Identifying literary forms
___ Identifying figures of speech
___ Distinguishing between fact and opinion
___ Distinguishing between fiction and nonfiction
___ Distinguishing between relevant and irrelevant information
___ Identifying cause and effect
___ Determining plot development
___ Following directions
___ Sequencing
___ Summarizing
___ Classifying ideas
___ Expanding language appreciation
___ Making associations
___ Forming generalizations
___ Drawing conclusions
___ Predicting outcomes
___ Making inferences
___ Making value judgements
___ Visualizing

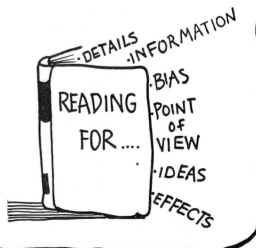

WRITING SKILLS CHECKLIST

Student's Name	Grade	Date	Teacher's Name

SKILLS   NOTES

- ____ Writing complete sentences
- ____ Using compound and complex sentences
- ____ Creating strong topic sentences
- ____ Adding details to support topic sentences
- ____ Choosing effective words
- ____ Using descriptive words
- ____ Sequencing ideas, events properly
- ____ Using a variety of sentence patterns
- ____ Developing plot effectively
- ____ Using appropriate style for given purpose
- ____ Using imagery
- ____ Writing effective beginnings and endings
- ____ Effectively setting a mood
- ____ Using sensory appeal
- ____ Creating emotional appeal
- ____ Writing for a specific audience
- ____ Expressing opinions and beliefs honestly
- ____ Outlining
- ____ Collecting and organizing ideas
- ____ Writing in the following forms:
    - ____ *Factual paragraphs*
    - ____ *2-3 paragraph reports*
    - ____ *Fictional paragraphs*
    - ____ *Short research reports*
    - ____ *Book reviews and reports*
    - ____ *Stories*
    - ____ *Arguments*
    - ____ *Announcements*
    - ____ *Conversations*
    - ____ *News articles, headlines, editorials*
    - ____ *Advertisements*
    - ____ *Summaries*
    - ____ *Letters and notes*
    - ____ *Short stories, fables, and tall tales*
    - ____ *Essays*
    - ____ *Autobiographies*
    - ____ *Biographies*
    - ____ *Descriptions*
    - ____ *Characterization*
    - ____ *Various forms of poetry*
    - ____ *Figures of speech*
    - ____ *Drama*

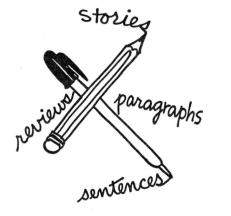

EDITING SKILLS CHECKLIST

Student's Name	Grade Date

Teacher's Name

SKILLS   NOTES

___ Substituting stronger (more colorful, more specific) words

___ Replacing inactive verbs with active ones

___ Eliminating redundancies

___ Rearranging words within a sentence

___ Expanding sentences to include more detail

___ Adding sentences to give more detail to a paragraph

___ Rearranging sentences for better clarity

___ Rearranging sentences for better sequencing

___ Rearranging sentences for a different meaning or sound

___ Making stronger titles

___ Changing endings

___ Creating smashing beginnings

___ Eliminating repetitive ideas or words

___ Eliminating unnecessary ideas or words

___ Breaking long sentences into shorter ones

___ Deciding if the written piece accomplishes the purpose

___ Adding words or phrases that create a certain mood, feeling

___ Varying sentence length and structure within a piece

___ Strengthening and varying transitions

___ Eliminating overused words, phrases, and cliche's

___ Replacing ordinary words with more interesting ones

___ Including words that convince

___ Adapting the content and form to a different audience

___ Changing outcomes by rearranging ideas

___ Adding dialogue to the piece

___ Adding understatement, exaggeration, foreshadowing, or irony to the piece

___ Including figures of speech

___ Varying rhymes and rhythms

___ Varying punctuation

___ Examining pieces for bias

___ Examining pieces for clarity

___ Examining pieces for effectiveness

___ Examining pieces to see that they appeal to the intended reader

The cunning detective sought clues.

STUDY SKILLS CHECKLIST

Student's Name   Grade   Date   Teacher's Name

SKILLS   NOTES

___ Identifying and using the following parts of a
book: table of contents, title page, copyright,
index, glossary, bibliography
___ Understanding dictionary format
___ Using a dictionary proficiently:
     ___ *Alphabetizing*
     ___ *Using guide words*
     ___ *Reading and understanding entries*
     ___ *Locating word meanings*
___ Locating reference materials
___ Choosing correct reference materials for a task
___ Using the following reference materials:
     ___ *Thesaurus*
     ___ *Encyclopedia*
     ___ *Atlas*
     ___ *Maps and globes*
     ___ *Charts, graphs and tables*
     ___ *Almanac*
     ___ *Periodicals*
     ___ *Newspapers*
     ___ *Time lines*
     ___ *Road atlas*
     ___ *Zip code directory*
     ___ *Telephone book (including Yellow Pages)*
     ___ *Footnotes*
___ Understanding the organization of a library
___ Locating books in the library
___ Using the card catalog
___ Showing proficiency in the following research
skills:
     ___ *Alphabetizing*
     ___ *Classifying*
     ___ *Following directions*
     ___ *Taking notes*
     ___ *Organizing information*
     ___ *Outlining*
     ___ *Summarizing*
     ___ *Locating details*
     ___ *Studying for a test*
     ___ *Taking a test*
     ___ *Interviewing*
     ___ *Skimming*

BRAINSTORMING GUIDE —

A GOOD WAY TO ENCOURAGE DIVERGENT THINKING

WHY?

The intended result of brainstorming is to generate a large number of ideas which will lead to a larger number of creative solutions to a given problem.

Two secondary benefits are derived from this process:
1. Students learn to express their ideas freely, without fear of criticism.
2. Students learn to build upon each other's ideas.

HOW?

There are four requirements for a profitable brainstorming session:
1. All ideas are accepted—defer judgement and criticism.
2. Participants must feel free to say everything they think and to hold nothing back. The "farther out" the ideas are, the better.
3. Participants build on the ideas of others. (Don't wait for a new idea to come. Let an idea grow out of the ideas already given by altering them in some way.)
4. Strive for quantity! The more ideas, the better.

FOLLOW-UP

After the brainstorming session:

1. Leave all ideas written as they were recorded.
2. Enlist student participation in setting standards for evaluating and pruning the collected ideas. (The criteria will depend on the intended use of the ideas.)
   - Examples: Is the idea practical?
     - Can we really accomplish it?
     - Is it compatible with everyday living?
     - Does it solve a problem without creating a new one?
3. Discuss which ideas fit the criteria.
4. Decide on ways to develop the ideas (making a model, diagram, design, drawing, writing descriptive material, etc.).

Adapted from SKILLSTUFF-REASONING, © 1981 by Incentive Publications, Inc., Nashville, TN.

PARTS OF SPEECH
An Activity For Champion Brainstormers

Can you think of ten originals for any of these? Try to think of ones that no one else has ever thought of, as far as you know!

four-lined rhymes
words (with their definitions)
holidays
subjects to study in school
ways to honor senior citizens
educational toys
colors
substitutes for shoes
rides for amusement parks
uses for peach pits
Halloween masks

flavors of ice cream
fast food restaurants
ways to serve potatoes
titles for songs
uses for ice cubes
recipes using chocolate
names for mystery novels
uses for an old calendar
T.V. situation comedies
games to play with three
   other people

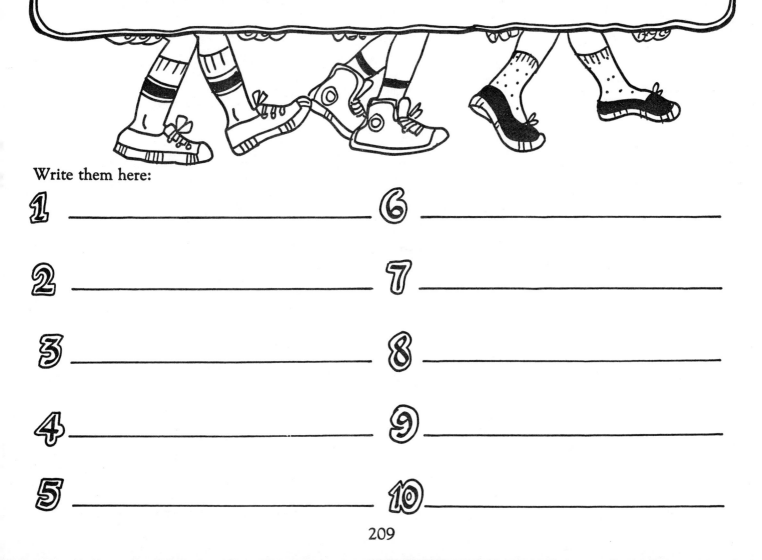

Write them here:

1 _____

2 _____

3 _____

4 _____

5 _____

6 _____

7 _____

8 _____

9 _____

10 _____

PARTS OF SPEECH

(AT-A-GLANCE GUIDE FOR YOUNG SPEAKERS & WRITERS)

IT'S CALLED...	THAT MEANS...	SUCH AS...
NOUN	The name of a person, place or thing.	Bobby, Sue, candy, monster, Miami, movie, July, box
PRONOUN	A word that takes the place of one or more nouns.	I, you, he, she, it, me, they, others, anyone, mine, yours, none, this, who
VERB	A word that expresses action or being.	swim, think, jump, smell, was, am, seem
ADJECTIVE	A word used to describe a noun.	silly, brave, huge, gross, purple, polka-dotted
ADVERB	A word used to describe a verb.	slowly, later, soon, very, suddenly, yesterday
PREPOSITION	A word that shows the relationship of a noun or pronoun to another word in the sentence.	ON the table, IN the drawer, FROM Daddy, OVER the rainbow
CONJUNCTION	A word that joins words or groups of words.	and, but, or
ARTICLE	The adjectives A, AN, THE.	a, an, the
INTERJECTION	An exclamatory word that expresses emotion. It stands alone -- away from the rest of the sentence.	Wow! Yikes! Ouch! Yeah! Horrors! Humbug!

MEET THE PUNCTUATION POWER FORCE

EMPLOYEES OF THE READING AND WRITING INDUSTRY

JOB DESCRIPTIONS:

PERIOD - To be used at the end of a sentence,
after numerals and letters in an outline,
after an abbreviation or initial.

EXCLAMATION POINT - To be used at the end of an
exclamatory sentence or a strong interjection.

QUESTION MARK - To be used at the end of an interrogative sentence.

COMMA - To separate items in a series,
direct quotations from the rest of a sentence,
days from months,and cities from states.
To appear after greetings, closings in letters and
any place that needs a short pause.

QUOTATION MARKS - To enclose the exact words of a speaker.
To set off titles of short stories, poems, articles,
chapters and songs.

APOSTROPHE - To show possession; to form contractions and plurals.

COLON - To introduce a list and
to help in writing time.

SEMICOLON - To separate the clauses of a compound sentence.

HYPHEN - To separate parts of words or
to come between parts of a compound adjective preceding a noun.

DASH - To mark a break in thought and
to announce a parenthetical thought or explanation.

HOW TO PREPARE A REPORT (PAPER, SPEECH, OR PROJECT)

1. CHOOSE A SUBJECT OR TOPIC . . . if possible, one in which you have some real interest!
2. MAKE A LIST OF SUBHEADINGS OR QUESTIONS to be answered about the topic:

   EX: Elephants   Japan
   - Description
   - Geographical location
   - Natural habitat
   - Habits
   - Relation to man
   - Pictures, maps, drawings, etc.

   - Location, geography, climate
   - History
   - People
   - Homes
   - Occupations
   - Pictures, maps, etc.

3. LOCATE REFERENCE MATERIALS -- resource books, pictures, drawings, artifacts.
4. RESEARCH EACH SUBTOPIC AND MAKE NOTES.
   (Don't try to write long sentences or paragraphs, yet. Just list information, to include later in more complete writing, in words, phrases and brief ideas. Use a different page for collecting notes on each subtopic.)
5. MAKE A LIST OF ALL REFERENCE MATERIALS USED. Be sure titles, authors, publishers and dates are accurate if you include a bibliography.
6. COLLECT SUPPORT MATERIALS -- pictures, drawings, maps, charts, artifacts, etc. -- that will complement or support the written information.
7. WRITE THE FIRST COPY. (Don't worry about proper form, spelling, handwriting, etc. Get the main ideas down. Be sure they relate to the topic and tell the story you want to tell.)

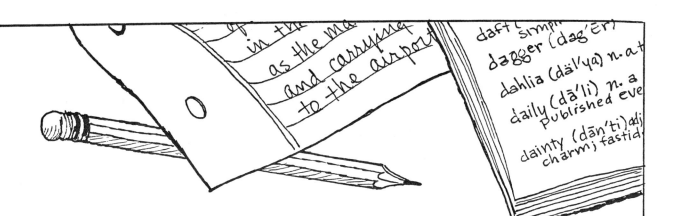

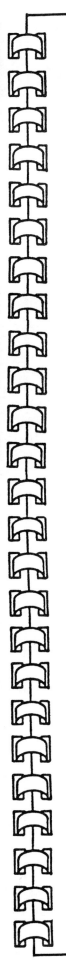

8. PROOFREAD AND EDIT THE FIRST COPY, using a dictionary and references to check data and spellings. Add or subtract parts as needed. (You can draw arrows and write in the margins to explain where new parts fit into the original copy.)

9. Now that you have everything you want to say on paper, you will be able to see how much space you will need.
   PLAN THE LAYOUT OF THE FINISHED WORK. Decide how and where you will add illustrations, maps, diagrams, demonstrations, etc.
   If you are doing an oral speech, you may want to transfer the work to cards and make an asterisk where you will use illustrations or demonstrations.
   If the finished work is to be written, plan the presentation so that it is as attractive and inviting as possible, and so that it meets any special requirements as to size or form.

10. WRITE OR TYPE YOUR FINAL COPY in neat, legible form.

11. ADD SUPPORT MATERIALS.

12. PREPARE THE BIBLIOGRAPHY, if needed.

13. CONGRATULATE YOURSELF on a job well done!

HOW TO STUDY FOR A TEST

1. FIND A PLACE TO WORK
2. GATHER ALL INFORMATION
3. ORGANIZE INFORMATION
4. MEMORIZE
5. SELF TEST
6. PARTNER TEST
7. "PHOTOGRAPH!"

1. Find a quiet, comfortable place (not too comfortable . . . preferably at a desk or table).
2. Gather textbooks, class notes, past quizzes, tests, lists, etc. -- all the information that may be tested.
3. Organize the information in LIST form on study sheets.

> (Generally speaking, rereading the text or class notes does not help very much . . . and information looks less scary when it's on a few pieces of paper!)
>
> Categorize your information and make lists of important facts and figures.
>
> If most information is in the textbook, underline the main headings, topics, and points to remember. Star the details you will need to memorize. Then, copy the information in list form on paper. Put the book aside. *

> EXAMPLE: Social Studies -- Make lists for categories such as:
> Names of People - their positions, contributions, etc.
> Important Events - why are they important?
> Important Dates
> Glossary of terms and definitions
> Miscellaneous
> (You may need to add a map. Mark key locations, topography, resources, etc.)

If there is a checkup or self test in the text, be sure to include those questions on your study sheet.

4. Memorize the lists! Think of tricks to help you remember.

    EXAMPLE: For remembering the Great Lakes, west to east:
           Smart   Men   Help   Each   Other
        (Superior - Michigan - Huron - Erie - Ontario)

        For spelling the word **geography**.
        George **El**liot's **o**ld **g**randfather **r**ode **a p**ig **h**ome **y**esterday.

5. Test yourself by covering the "answer" half of your list OR by quickly scribbling out a "test" for yourself. Drill yourself until you think you have it.
6. Give your notes to a parent or friend who will ask you the questions and help you remember answers when you forget.
7. "Photograph" your study sheets with your mind's eye. Try to remember how they look. Picture where the information is located on the paper. (Some kids say that doing this just before you go to sleep the night before the test is the way to a sure "A"!)

HOW TO TAKE A TEST

1. Be prepared with the proper tools (pen, pencils, erasers, etc.).

2. Relax! (Close your eyes, sit back and relax your entire body. Let your head and limbs droop. Breathe slowly in and out to the count of ten. Then, sit up in an alert, comfortable position.)

3. Write your name at the top of the test paper. Then, skim the *entire* test.

4. Starting at the beginning, go through the test answering all the items you can answer easily and quickly.

5. Go back to the beginning and answer those questions which are more difficult. (If certain difficult items are worth more points than others, do those items ahead of the single-point items.)

6. Try to use time wisely. Do not allow yourself to spend too much time on any one item.

7. NEVER hand in a test early (before the required time) unless you have reread the entire test and rechecked every answer carefully. Careless mistakes cost points . . . and there's only one point difference between an "A" and a "B" . . . or between a "D" and an "F"!

8. As soon as your paper is in and you're out of the classroom, shout a loud "HURRAY!" Smile . . . it's over!

IDIOMS

She bawled her eyes out.
My brother gets in my hair.
He lost his marbles.
The idea rang a bell.
He was burned up.
Go fly a kite.
He almost bit my head off!
She blew her stack.
He's on top of the world.
She is as quiet as a church mouse.
He's as neat as a pin.
The baby is prettier than a picture.
He's like a bull in a china shop.
That will take him down a peg.
Dad will get wind of it.
Money always burns a hole in my pocket.
Will you lend me a hand?
She was so nervous she blew the test.
I was so scared, I was shaking in my boots.
The girl was walking on air after the dance.
I was furious, but I held my tongue.
I'm between the devil and the deep blue sea.
He's not worth a hill of beans.
I think he bit off more than he can chew.
It's raining cats and dogs out there!
He has a trick up his sleeve.
It's as plain as the nose on your face.
I'm in a pretty pickle!
Do you have a skeleton in your closet?
The handwriting was on the wall.
I'd be tickled pink to see her again.
With this money, I'll be on Easy Street.
I broke the window, and I'm in hot water now!
He bought the company and then lost his shirt.
After the accident, things were touch and go.
You have to make hay while the sun shines.
What I say to him goes in one ear and out the
    other.
Don't make a mountain out of a molehill.
I'll keep my eye on the baby for you.
The dead fish smelled to high heaven.
I saw the snake and almost jumped out of my
    skin.
To clean that dirty oven, I have to use lots of
    elbow grease.
He cried wolf one too many times.
Don't cry over spilt milk.
You're skating on thin ice when you tell your
    mother a lie.
Are you getting cold feet about asking for more
    money?
Many sailors have gone to Davy Jones's locker.
There are several forks in that road.

You must have rocks in your head.
I'm coming, so keep your shirt on.
He's talking through his hat.
That's right down my alley.
He is a pain in the neck.
The cowboy bit the dust.
He's as nutty as a fruitcake.
I have a splitting headache.
Put your John Hancock on the paper.
I never see eye to eye with you.
Is she ever in the dumps!
For crying out loud, stop that noise.
I have a bone to pick with you!
She really can chew the fat.
You just hit the nail on the head.
By hook or by crook I'll get it.
That rings a bell with me.
The judge will throw the book at him.
It's nothing to shake a stick at.
Hold your horses!
I just had to blow off steam.
Keep a stiff upper lip.
I believe she is full of beans.
The teacher called him on the carpet.
That is as easy as rolling off a log.
I've got to get forty winks.
He has too many irons in the fire.
She's as mad as a wet hen.
It is not fake, it's the real McCoy.
You're in the doghouse now!
That is just a drop in the bucket.
The doctor says I'm fit as a fiddle.
She has a frog in her throat.
You are driving me up the wall.

YOU ARE DRIVING
ME UP THE
WALL!

Adapted from SKILLSTUFF - READING © 1979 by Incentive Publications, Inc.

GOOD VOCABULARY
WORDS TO LEARN

abet
abomination
abduct
acclaim
affluent
allegory
allude
aloof
ambiance
analogy
anecdote
apparition
arduous
audacious
averse

bamboozle
barbarian
befuddle
bellow
benevolent
beneficiary
bestial
blatant
banish
boor
botch
bungle

calamity
capitulate
censure
certitude
chasten
circumspect
cleave
commiserate
complacent
comply
conjecture
consequence
cornice
crass
credible

dauntless
decorum
deem
default

deliberate
delirium
demur
depreciate
despondent
deviate
dilapidated
discreet
disparage
distend
duplicity

eccentric
edifice
effervescent
efficient
ego
eminent
encore
ensign
epitome
erratic
eulogy
exasperate
excruciating
exorbitant
expound

fallacious
feasible
fervent
figment
filch
flagrant
flippant
forebear
forelock
forlorn
fraudulent
fraught
frenzy
fugitive
furtive

gallant
galoshes
gape
garble
garnish

garrulous
gauche
gazebo
glean
gnash
gourmet
gusto

haggard
haughty
heckle
heinous
hoard
hype
hyperbole
hypocrite

illusion
impasse
impervious
impudent
inaugurate
indolent
induce
indulge
inept
infuriate
insipid
insinuate
integrity
intrepid
intuition
irrational

jeopardy
jovial
juvenile

kin
kindred
knack
knave

labrinth
lackadaisical
lament
languish
leisure
lenient

lethargy
listless
lithe
loiter
loquacious
luminous

macabre
maelstrom
malice
mandate
marinade
martial
meander
meddle
melancholy
menial
mesmerize
metropolis
mocha
monument
mutiny
mystic

naive
nebulous
nimble
nominee
noxious
novice
nudge

oblige
obscure
obstruct
obstinate
odious
ominous
oppress
orifice
oscitancy

palatable
pallid
pandemonium
parable
parcel
perpetual
phenomenon
pious

placate
placid
poignant
precarious
predicament
prosper
proximity
pulsate

qualm
quandary
query
quip

rational
rebellion
recede
recluse
recurrence
refute
regimen
renounce
repudiate
repugnant
resplendent
retaliate
retort
rigid
rigor
rogue

satire
savor
scholastic
scruple
sedition
semblance
serpentine
servile
shirk
simulate
skeptic
snare
sojourn
soothsayer
spontaneous
spurious
subordinate
suffrage

sullen

taunt
technical
tedious
terminal
theory
tier
timorous
titanic
tolerant
toxic
tranquil
transient
truce
turbid
turgid

ultimate
universal
usage
utopia

vacate
vacuous
vagabond
valid
valor
vanquish
varigated
venomous
vestibule
vicious
villain
virtuoso
visage
voracious

waft
wane
warrant
wary
wince
woebegone
wrangle

zealot
zenith
zest

PREFIXES/SUFFIXES/ROOTS

a	able	act
ab	age	port
ante	ar	sense
anti	al	love
auto	ance	dark
bi	er	science
circu	ery	teach
co	est	dark
con	ful	wonder
counter	fy	fear
de	hood	difference
dis	ible	kind
ex	ic	arrange
extra	ion	study
fore	ish	read
il	ist	print
im	ity	community
in	ive	zero
inter	kess	star
ir	ly	date
mid	ment	possible
mis	most	true
non	ness	honest
oct	or	friend
over	ous	polite
post	ship	behave
pre	tion	fortune
pro	ure	move
quart	y	view
re		cycle
sub		form
super		
tele		
trans		
tri		
un		
uni		

super   polite   ly

MEANINGS OF PREFIXES/ SUFFIXES

PREFIXES

ante	before	antecede
anti	against	antiwar
bi	two, twice	biweekly
co	together, with	copilot
counter	against	counterattack
de	down, away	descend
dis	not	displease
ex	out	export
fore	in front	foreground
in	not	incorrect
ir	not	irregular
mid	middle	midway
mis	wrong	misread
non	not	nonstop
post	after	postdate
pre	before, in front	preview
re	again	rewrite
sub	under	subway
tele	far away	telephone
trans	across	transatlantic
un	not	unkind

SUFFIXES

ance	state of being	importance
ar	one who does something	liar
en	having nature of	golden
er	one who does something	baker
ery	place which	bakery
full	full of	successful
fy	form into	beautify
hood	state or rank	statehood
ible	able to	visible
ic	like, pertaining to	dramatic
ion	act, process of	action
ish	having nature of	wolfish
ist	one who	artist
less	without	toothless
ly	in the manner of	lovely
ment	action or process	payment
ness	state of being	friendliness
or	one who does something	actor
ous	state or condition	famous
ship	office or skill	championship
tion	act, process of	education

ABBREVIATIONS

A.D.	Anno Domini, in the year of our Lord
A.M., a.m.	ante meridiem, before noon
anon.	anonymous
assoc.	associate; associated
asst.	assistant
atty.	attorney
B.A.	Bachelor of Arts
B.C.	Before Christ; British Columbia
bros.	brothers
C	Centigrade; Celcius
cal.	calories
cap.	capital
cent.	century
ch., chap.	chapter
cm.	centimeter
c/o	care of
co.	company; county
c.o.d.	cash on delivery collect on delivery
cont.	continued
cop, ©	copyright
corp.	corporation
C.S.T.	Central Standard Time
D.A.	District Attorney
DDT	dichloro-diphenyl-trichloroethane
dm.	decimeter
D.S.T	Daylight Saving Time
ed.	edition
enc.	enclosure; encyclopedia
Esq.	Esquire
E.S.T.	Eastern Standard Time
F	Fahrenheit
FBI	Federal Bureau of Investigation
FDA	Food and Drug Administration
Fr.	Father; Friar; French
ft.	feet; foot; fort
gal.	gallon
Gov.	Governor
govt.	government
grad.	graduate; graduated
gr.	gram
Hon.	Honorable
ht.	height; heat
I., i.	island
ibid.	ibidem, in the same place
inc.	incorporated; including
in.	inch
I.O.U.	I owe you
I.Q.	intelligence quotient
kg.	kilogram
km.	kilometer
l.	liter
lat.	latitude
lb.	pound
liq.	liquid
lit.	literature
Lt., Lieut.	Lieutenant
Ltd., Lim.	Limited

m.	meter
M.A.	Master of Arts
M.D.	Doctor of Medicine
meas.	measure
misc.	miscellaneous
Mlle.	Mademoiselle
mi.	mile
mm.	millimeter
Mme.	Madame
mo.	month
Msgr.	Monsignor
M.S.T.	Mountain Standard Time
n.	noun; north
nat., natl.	national
NATO	North Atlantic Treaty Organization
no.	number
oz.	ounce
p.	page
par.	paragraph; parenthesis
pd.	paid
Ph.D.	Doctor of Philosophy
philos.	philosophy
pk.	park; peak; peck
pl.	plural; place; plate
P.M., p.m.	post meridiem, after noon; postmaster; post mortem
P.O.	post office
pop.	population
POW	prisoner of war
ppd.	prepaid
prin.	principal
Prov.	Proverbs
P.S.	post scriptum, postscript
P.S.T.	Pacific Standard Time
pt.	pint
qt.	quart
rd.	road
Rev.	Reverend; Revelations
rev.	review; revise; revolution
R.R.	railroad
R.S.V.P.	Answer, if you please
sch.	school
sec.	second
sig.	signature
sing.	singular
sp.	spelling; species; space
spec.	specification
sq.	square
Sr.	Senior
St.	Saint; strait; street
subj.	subject
t.	ton
tech.	technical; technology
treas.	treasurer
UN	United Nations
v.	verb
v, vs	versus, against
VIP	Very Important Person
vol.	volume
wt.	weight
yd.	yard
yr.	year

HOMONYMS

aid, ade, aide
aisle, isle, I'll
alter, altar
bare, bear
be, bee
beat, beet
beech, beach
berry, bury
boll, bowl,
blue, blew
bore, boar
bough, bow
break, brake
bye, buy, by
capital, capitol
carrot, carat
cereal, serial
coarse, course
compliment, complement
council, counsel
creek, creak
dear, deer
elusive, illusive
fair, fare
feet, feat
flour, flower
fourth, forth
gorilla, guerilla
great, grate
groan, grown
idle, idol
hair, hare
knows, nose
leek, leak
liar, lyre
loan, lone
low, lo
maid, made
mail, male
mettle, metal
meet, meat
minor, miner
mousse, moose
navel, naval
need, knead
new, gnu, knew
none, nun
not, knot
our, hour
pain, pane

palate, pallet
peace, piece
peel, peal
plain, plane
presence, presents
prey, pray
principal, principle
raise, raze
read, reed
real, reel
red, read
reign, rein, rain
right, write, rite
ring, wring
sail, sale
seam, seem
seen, scene
sell, cell
sense, cents, scents
serf, surf
slay, sleigh
soar, sore
so, sew
sole, soul
some, sum
son, sun
stake, steak
stare, stair
stationery, stationary
straight, strait
tale, tail
tax, tacks
tear, tier
there, they're
through, threw
thyme, time
to, two, too
toe, tow
troupe, troop
vein, vain, vane
wait, weight
waste, waist
wave, waive
way, weigh
weak, week
whole, hole
won, one
wood, would
wry, rye
you, ewe, yew

ANTONYMS

above	below	absent	present
add	subtract	love	hate
alike	different	ancient	new
arid	wet	asleep	awake
begin	finish	below	above
descend	ascend	blunt	sharp
fearful	courageous	tranquil	chaotic
asset	liability	delete	add
reject	accept	praise	criticize
funny	serious	damage	repair
perilous	safe	deep	shallow
difficult	easy	gather	disperse
succeed	fail	catch	throw
busy	idle	well	ill
imaginary	real	innocent	guilty
later	sooner	loose	tight
harsh	gentle	strength	weakness
noisy	quiet	open	closed
pain	pleasure	peace	war
assent	dissent	rebel	comply
polite	rude	poverty	wealth
raise	lower	present	absent
rough	smooth	sell	purchase
frown	smile	several	few
listen	ignore	accelerate	decelerate
punctual	tardy	false	true
rare	common	tame	wild
straight	crooked	narrow	wide
calm	anxious	distasteful	delicious
compliment	insult	joyful	grouchy
disagreeable	agreeable	interesting	boring
sweet	sour	simple	complicated
minor	adult	create	destroy
schedule	cancel	backward	forward

GLOSSARY OF WRITING TERMS

Allegory—a story presented on a superficial level which parallels and illustrates a deeper meaning.

Alliteration—the repetition of one initial sound in several words within a phrase.

Annotation—a short, critical commentary of a book.

Ballad—a narrative poem which uses simple language and a refrain, is usually intended to be sung, and is often a folk tale.

Bibliography—a formal listing of books, usually on a specific subject, giving author, title, city, publisher, and date.

Characterization—the description of a person through the use of any of a variety of literary techniques.

Cinquain— a five-lined poetic form which follows this pattern: line 1, a one-word subject or idea; line 2, two descriptive adjectives; line 3, three related action verbs; line 4, three or four words that give a personal reaction; line 5, a one-word synonym for the first line.

Cliché—a trite, overused expression.

Climax—the point at which a story, poem, or drama reaches its most intense, emotional point; culmination.

Colloquialism—an informal, conversational word or phrase which may be idiomatic or may include slang and/or jargon native to a certain locality or region.

Couplet—a two-lined poetic form in which both lines use the same rhyme scheme and meter.

Dialogue—the conversation between two or more characters.

Diamante—a seven-lined poetic form which follows this pattern: lines 1 and 7, a noun or pronoun; lines 2 and 6, two adjectives; lines 3 and 5, three participles; line 4, four nouns.

Edit—to prepare a manuscript, book, article, etc. for publication by correcting and polishing it.

Editorial—a newspaper article which usually expresses the editor's view (or another person's view) on a current situation.

Epic—an extensive narrative poem which celebrates an event or praises the adventures of a hero/heroine who is important to the history of a culture group.

Epigraph—a quotation or motto, found at the beginning of a chapter or a book, which is related to the material that follows it.

Epilogue—a short speech made directly to the audience at the end of a play, or a concluding section at the end of a literary work which usually deals with the future of the characters from that work.

Epitaph—a short literary piece epitomizing and praising a deceased person.

Essay—a short, personal literary composition which usually gives the views of the writer.

Expository—a kind of writing in which meaning or intent is clearly stated.

Fable—a story about legendary people and events.

Figure of Speech—an expression using words in an unusual sense to add vividness or drama.

First Draft—the first written form of a literary work.

Flashback—an explanatory episode which interrupts a play or story to show something that happened in the past.

Footnote—a note found at the bottom of a page which cites a reference for a designated part of the text.

Free Verse—poetry which follows no conventional rhythm pattern or rhyme scheme.

Glossary—a listing in the back of a book in which words are defined in terms of their usage within that book.

Haiku—a Japanese poetic form which consists of three lines; the first and third having five syllables, and the second having seven syllables.

Idiom—a phrase that conveys a meaning different from the exact definitions of the words used in it.

Imagery—the employment of figures of speech or vivid descriptions; the collection of such representations in a literary work.

Index—an alphabetical listing of terms in a book, accompanied by the page numbers on which each is found.

Irony—an expression which makes a deliberate contrast between what appears to be so and what actually is.

Jargon—the specialized language of a group, profession, or fellowship of some sort.

Journal—a daily record; diary.

Legend—an unverified, popular narrative story handed down from the past.

Limerick—a five-lined, light, nonsensical or humorous verse which usually uses the rhyme scheme a-a-b-b-a.

Lyric—poetry which is melodic in form and personal and sensual in nature.

Metaphor—a figure of speech that implies comparison between two things which are basically unlike.

Monologue—a speech in which there is only one speaker.

Mood—the feeling that a composition produces in its reader.

Myth—a story which originated in a preliterate society, usually dealing with supernatural beings or heroes/heroines.

Narrative—a story or description of events.

Ode—a long, lyric poem, often rhymed, that usually addresses and praises in exalted terms some person, object, or quality.

Onomatopoeia—the formation of a word by imitating the sound associated with the object or action.

Outline—a formal summarization of information that follows a definite, grammatical format.

Parable—a simple story which illustrates a moral or religious truth.

Parody—a work that intentionally and broadly mimics, and thereby ridicules, the characteristic work of another.

Personification—the act of endowing an inanimate object or abstraction with human qualities.

Plot—a series of events which makes up the outline or action of a literary work.

Point of View—the position from which something is told; the narrator's position.

Précis—a concise summary of the essential facts; writing which is very concise and to the point.

Prologue—the poetry or prose that introduces a play or a narrative, usually set off from the main body of the work.

Proofread—to carefully check a written work for errors.

Pun—a literary form which is a play on words, either on a word which has several meanings, or on words that sound alike.

Quatrain—a four-lined stanza or poem which usually has a rhymed pattern.

Report—a detailed account of information or an event presented in a formal, organized format.

Review—a critical work (usually in written form) which reports on a book, a play, or some form of entertainment.

Rhyme Scheme—any of various rhyming patterns used in poetry.

Satire—a literary work of any form which employs wit, derision, or irony to point out and ridicule folly, stupidity, or sin.

Script—the written text of a play, show, or movie.

Simile—a figure of speech, introduced by *like* or *as*, in which two things are compared.

Sonnet—a poem, composed of an octave (8 lines) and a sestet (6 lines), in which the complete statement and resolution of a theme are related.

Spoonerism—an unintentional transposition of sounds in spoken language.

Summary—a condensed, concise re-statement of information.

Tanka—a Japanese verse form of five lines in which the first and third lines have five syllables and all others have seven syllables.

Vignette—a delicate, subtle, literary sketch; a decorative design sometimes found at the beginning or end of a chapter or a book.

Vocabulary—all the words used and understood by a person or a group.

TRY WRITING THESE . . .

ads (for magazines, newspapers, Yellow Pages)
advice columns
allegories
anecdotes
announcements
anthems
appendices
apologies
assumptions
autobiographies
awards

ballads
beauty tips
bedtime stories
beginnings
billboards
biographies
blurbs
books
book jackets
book reviews
brochures
bulletins
bumper stickers

calendar quips
calorie charts
campaign speeches
cartoons
captions
catalog entries
cereal boxes
certificates
character sketches
church bulletins
community bulletins
couplets
comparisons
comic strips
complaints
constitutions
contracts
conundrums
conversations
critiques
crossword puzzles
cumulative stories

data sheets
definitions
descriptions
dialogues
diaries
diets
directions
directories
documents
double talk
dramas
dream scripts

editorials
epilogues
epitaphs
encyclopedia entries
endings
essays
evaluations
exaggerations
exclamations
explanations

fables
fairy tales
fantasies
fashion articles
fashion show scripts
folklore
fortunes

gags
game rules
graffiti
good news/bad news
greeting cards
grocery lists
gossip

headlines
horoscopes
how-to-do-it speeches
hymns

impromptu speeches

indexes
inquiries
insults
interviews
introductions (to people, places, books)
invitations

jingles
job applications
jokes
journals
jump rope rhymes

labels
legends
letters
lies
lists
love notes
luscious words
lyrics

magazines
malapropisms
marquee notices
memories
metaphors
menus
monologues
movie reviews
movie scripts
mysteries
myths

news analyses
newscasts
newspapers
nonsense
notebooks
nursery rhymes

obituaries
observations
odes
opinions

palindromes
pamphlets

parodies
party tips
persuasive letters
phrases
plays
poems
post cards
posters
prayers
predictions
problems
problem solutions
proformas
profound sayings
prologues
proposals
propaganda sheets
protest signs
protest letters
product descriptions
proverbs
puppet shows
puns
puzzles

questionnaires
questions
quips
quizzes
quotations

ransom notes
reactions
real estate notices
rebuttals
recipes
record covers

remedies
reports
requests
Requiems
requisitions
resumés
reviews
revisions
rhymes
riddles

sale notices
sales pitches
satires
schedules
secrets
self-portraits
sentences
sequels
serialized stories
sermons
signs
silly sayings
skywriting messages
slogans
soap operas
society news
songs
speeches
spoofs
spook stories
spoonerisms
sports accounts
sports analyses

superstitions

T.V. commercials
T.V. guides
T.V. programs
tall tales
telegrams
telephone directory
textbooks
thank you notes
theater programs
titles
tongue twisters
traffic rules
transcripts
travel folders
travel posters
tributes
trivia

used car descriptions

vignettes
vitas

want ads
wanted posters
warnings
wills
wise sayings
wishes
weather reports
weather forecasts
WORDS

yarns
Yellow Pages

Adapted from IF YOU'RE TRYING TO TEACH KIDS HOW TO WRITE, © 1979 by Incentive Publications, Inc., Nashville, TN.

PLAN FOR INDIVIDUALIZED READING

1 Choose a book. Check the difficulty of the book by using the difficulty rule of thumb.

RULE OF THUMB

When you select a book, turn to the middle and read silently. Put your thumb on the table. Each time you miss a word, put a finger down. If you put all of your fingers down while reading on that one page, the book is too difficult.

2 Each day, fill in your reading log. Write the date, the title of the book, the pages read, and any difficult vocabulary words. Ask for help if you cannot find the words in the dictionary. DO NOT SKIP THEM!

3 You will have conferences on the books you read. Write your name on the board when you are finished with the book to sign up for a conference.

4 Choose a few paragraphs to share with your teacher. Practice reading them before your conference.

5 Each book must be followed up with an activity of your choice from the "Great Ways To Share A Book" sheet, or you may discuss an original project idea with the teacher.

6 During the sharing time, you may share parts of your book and your completed project with others.

7 Keep your reading log and written assignments in your reading folder. Bring your folder and book to each conference.

8 Each time you finish a book, fill in a section on your "Ring-Around-Reading Record" (232). When your circle is full, ask your teacher for your *reading reward* and start a new circle.

INDIVIDUAL READING CONFERENCE CHECK SHEET

NAME: **DATES:**

Title	Type of Book	Level	Fluency	Word Attack Skills	Comprehensive

Notes:

Title	Type of Book	Level	Fluency	Word Attack Skills	Comprehensive

Notes:

Title	Type of Book	Level	Fluency	Word Attack Skills	Comprehensive

Notes:

RING-AROUND-READING RECORD

Fill in the spokes of the Ring-Around-Reading Record. As you read a book from each category, write the name and author of the book and the date you completed it in the spoke. Use felt-tip pens to color the spokes.

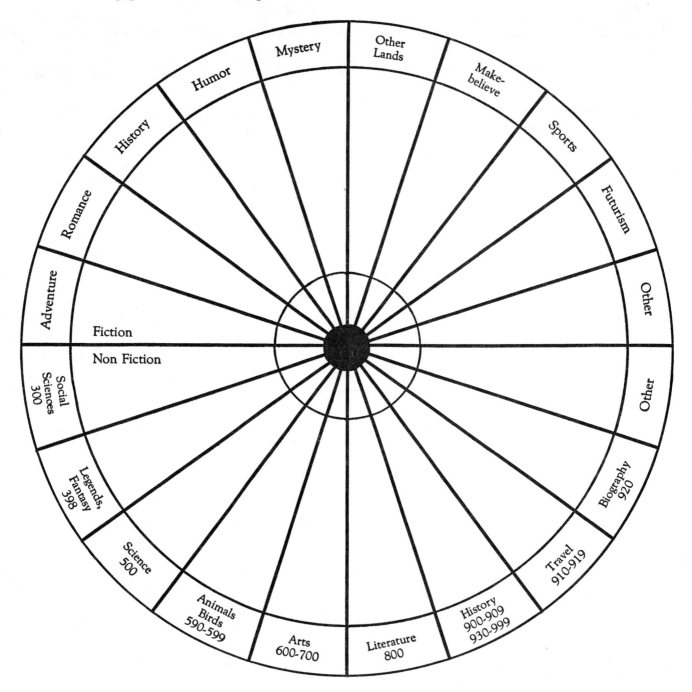

Name: _____

Date Finished: _____

My Reading Log

NAME:

ONE SUMMER I READ 44 BOOKS AND ATE 3.

Date	Title of Book	Pages Read	New and Different Words
1.			
2.			
3.			
4.			
5.			
6.			
7.			
8.			
9.			

MY PLAN FOR A READING PROJECT

Name _____ Beginning Date _____ Completion Date _____

Title of project: _____

Project description (what I want to find out and why): _____

_____

_____

_____

_____

_____

_____

_____

_____

Materials I will need (including reference books): _____

_____

_____

_____

Plans for carrying out project: _____

_____

_____

_____

How I will report or share my findings: _____

_____

_____

_____

GREAT WAYS TO SHARE A BOOK

- Make a crossword puzzle using ideas from a book. Give it to someone who has read the book. Make enough copies to keep on hand for others who read the book.

- Read a book that has been made into a movie. Write an essay comparing the movie with the book.

- Rewrite the story as a picture book. Use simple vocabulary so that the book may be enjoyed by younger students.

- Suggest some changes which you think the author might make in order to improve the book.

- Dress up as one of the characters and tell the story from a first person viewpoint.

- After reading a book about history or an historical fiction, make a time line or calendar to show the important events of the story.

- Prepare a list of questions for use in determining if others have read the book carefully.

- Write a description of one of the main characters. Paint a portrait or caricature to accompany the description.

- Make three or four simple puppets of characters in the book. Prepare a short puppet show to tell the story to the class.

- Write a letter to the school librarian telling why she or he should recommend the book to other classes.

- Compare the illustrations in two books. Tell how the illustrations influence the reader.

- After reading a factual book, make a list of ten important facts you found in the book.

- Write a book review to be printed in the school newspaper.

- Write a letter to the author of your book, telling your feelings about the story. Mail the letter to the book's publishing company.

- Make a map showing where the story took place.

- Write a diary from the main character's viewpoint to explain the events of the story.

- Make up three different endings for the story.

- Write a letter recommending the book to a friend or relative in another city.

- Make a list of questions to ask someone who has read the same book. Then, interview that person and record his or her answers on tape.

- Write a letter to the main character of your book. (Ask a question, protest some situation, make a complaint or suggestion, etc.)

- Write a feature news article (with a headline) that tells the story as it might be found on the front page of a newspaper in the town where the story takes place.

- Draw several illustrations to accompany the book. Be prepared to tell the story to the class, using the pictures as aids.

- Make a travel poster inviting tourists to visit the setting of the book.

- If your book is a poetry book, make a scrapbook containing 15 or 20 of your favorite poems.

- After reading a joke and riddle book, make a scrapbook of original jokes and riddles.

- Make a *diorama* which shows the setting of a main event from the book.

- Make a poster which advertises your book.

CREATIVE OUT-OF-SCHOOL ACTIVITIES

1. Ask every member of your family to choose one T.V. program for the whole family to watch sometime during the week. Plan a time for family members to vote by secret ballot for the best program and to discuss why the particular programs were selected (entertainment, educational value, graphic or dramatic presentation, etc.). Write summaries of the programs watched, your evaluation of each, and the chief benefits of the experience for your family.

2. Select 20 words that you would like to add to your speaking and/or writing vocabulary. Desgin a word find puzzle using the 20 words. Add your completed puzzle to the class collection.

3. Interview a senior citizen whom you admire. Ask questions designed to acquire interesting anecdotes as well as pertinent facts. Use your notes to write the person's biography.

4. Select a hobby that interests you. Use reference books and conferences with resource people to research the topic as thoroughly as possible. Prepare an outline for a 10 to 15 minute, oral report on the expenditures of time and money necessary to pursue the hobby and the advantages and disadvantages associated with the hobby. Present your report to the class.

5. Save all the "junk mail" that comes to your house for one week. Classify the mail in at least 15 different ways. (Try for 25 ways if you want to be a really "classy classificationist".) Make a list of ten to 20 words or phrases used to persuade the receiver to take the action desired by the sender. Choose the advertisement that you think does the best job of presenting the product to make you feel that you just can't live without it. Try to determine what techniques make the ad successful.

6. Write ten good questions (with answers, of course) for a "factual pursuit" game about your community, state or nation.

7. Devise a questionnaire to find out which persons in your neighborhood read a lot. Then interview at least ten people of different age groups who read often. Use your "findings" to make a neighborhood "most read" book list.

8. Read the want ads in your daily newspaper to find out what jobs in your community are in the most demand. Select one job that you think you might like to have ten years from now, and list the qualifications, benefits and starting salary. Write a resume' to submit to a prospective employer represented by one of the ads in the newspaper.

9. Select three full-page magazine ads that do an especially good job of presenting the product or service offered. List six key words from each that help to make the "sales pitch". Underline the words that appear in more than one ad. Add six words of your own that could be used to make the ad more effective.

10. Design a new board game which will help you review your weekly spelling or vocabulary words.

11. Read one front page news story in three different newspapers. Write a paragraph to present the similarities and differences in the three accounts.

12. Choose one advertisement in your local newspaper that you feel oversells the product. Rewrite the ad to make the description of the product more accurate.

13. Select a book to read to a younger child. Keep in mind the child's age and comprehension level, as well as his or her interests. Read the book aloud to the child. Was the topic interesting enough to hold the child's attention? Were the illustrations colorful and commanding?

14. Write a letter to a local or national politician stating your views on a topic of concern to you. Mail your letter and wait to find out how promptly it will be answered.

15. Choose a topic related to the current welfare of human beings and make a poster to encourage awareness of this topic.

16. Select a vacation site that you would like to visit. Use travel brochures, magazines, interviews with people who have visited the site, and reference books to secure as much information as possible. Design an original travel brochure to present your findings. Include specifics related to location, climate, scenic and cultural features, available accomodations and costs for lodging and transportation.

Other KIDS' STUFF books for Middle Grades
Language Arts and Reading

Edwards, Candy. **The Reference Point**. 1983.
- a collection of reproducible pages, learning centers and teaching suggestions that help develop and strengthen important library skills.

Forte, Imogene. **Library & Reference Bulletin Boards**. 1986.
- motivational bulletin boards with patterns and additional captions.

Forte, Imogene. **Read About It Middle Grades**. 1982.
- reproducible activities which focus on word recognition, word usage and independent reading skills.

Forte, Imogene. **Think About It Middle Grades**. 1981.
- reproducible activity sheets designed to develop thinking skills such as discovering, predicting, inventing, interpreting, imagining and more.

Forte, Imogene. **Write About It Middle Grades**. 1983.
- reproducible worksheets which focus on vocabulary development, technical writing, composition and original writing.

Forte, Imogene. **Skillstuff: Reading**. 1979.
- word recognition and usage, comprehension and study skills.

Forte, Imogene and MacKenzie, Joy. **Skillstuff: Reasoning**. 1981.
- comprehension, application, analysis, synthesis and evaluation skills and processes.

Forte, Imogene and MacKenzie, Joy. **Skillstuff: Writing**. 1980.
- using words and phrases; technical writing, composition and original writing; life skills.

Forte, Imogene and Pangle, Mary Ann. **Reading Bulletin Boards**. 1986.
- includes skills-based activities to supplement daily reading programs.

Frank, Marjorie. **If You're Trying To Teach Kids How To Write, You've Gotta Have This Book**. 1979.
- a how-to book for understanding and working with the whole writing process with ideas for specific activities and suggestions for solving writing problems.

Richards, Joanne and Standley, Marianne. **One For The Books**. 1984.
- original and creative ways to present book reports.

Richards, Joanne and Standley, Marianne. **Write Here**. 1984.
- includes writing activities, bulletin boards and suggestions for motivating students.

The Yellow Pages For Students and Teachers. 1980.
- a book of reference lists for teaching basic reading, writing and thinking skills.

MISSING LINKS

You've heard of the "missing link," but you probably never expected to find it hidden in the pages of a reference book!

Each name listed below is really a combination of two names. To find the "missing link," try to discover the name that goes between the two names and fits with both.

EXAMPLE: Babe Saint Denis
The missing link is RUTH.
Babe Ruth and Ruth Saint Denis

Since many names will not be familiar to you, you will need to look up the names in an encyclopedia or other reference book containing names. If there is more than one entry for a last name, experiment by inserting different first names.

TRY THESE!

1. William O. MacArthur
2. Benjamin Roosevelt
3. Sarah Ste. Antoinette
4. Sir Walter Carpenter
5. Sinclair Carroll
6. Patrick Ford
7. Prince de Gaulle
8. O. Kissinger
9. Booker T. Irving
10. Anne Lloyd Wright

• See answers on page 240.

Create some missing links of your own on the back of this page!

BORDER PUZZLE

Each set of "squiggly" lines below represents segments of the borders between three or more states. Use your atlas to identify each group of states and label them correctly.

For answers, see page 240.

Create some additional border puzzles of your own. See if your classmates can identify them.

HEADLINE HEROES

• See answers on page 240.

IF TIME IS SO SHORT, WHY ARE TIME LINES SO LONG?

Use reference materials to locate the dates on which these events took place.

Beethoven's birth
Emancipation Proclamation signed
Ratification of U.S. Constitution
Attack on Pearl Harbor Day
Monroe Doctrine signed
First American in space
Paul Revere's ride
End of World War II
Elizabeth II crowned queen
First pilgrims land at Plymouth
President Washington's inauguration
Richard M. Nixon resigned
Discovery of gold in California
Boston Tea Party
J.F. Kennedy assassinated
President Lincoln's inauguration
Man's first walk on moon
William Shakespeare's birth

• See page 240 for answers.

HISTORIC MOMENTS MYSTERY

Use the "clue" words, your encyclopedia and other reference books to pinpoint the historic event that took place and the year.

CLUE WORDS	EVENT	DATE
1. THREE · PINTA · LAND HO!	Columbus Discovers America	1492
2. BROTHERS · KITTY · WINGS		
3. CHEESE · STEP · ARMSTRONG		
4. HELEN'S · ERUPT · ASHES		
5. ROCK · PILGRIMS · MAYFLOWER		
6. FREE · PROCLAMATION · SLAVES		
7. ALOHA · 50 · STATEHOOD		
8. BOOTH · THEATER · PRESIDENT		
9. PEARL · JAPAN · SURPRISE		
10. DOCUMENT · TEN · RIGHTS		
11. REVERE · ALARM · RIDE		
12. STOCKS · PANIC · CRASH		
13. PENICILLIN · FLEMING · MOLD		
14. PARTY · TAXES · BOSTON		
15. ICEBERG · NORTH ATLANTIC · UNSINKABLE		

• See page 240 for answers.

WHERE IT'S ALWAYS CHRISTMAS

Did you know . . . it's always Christmas in Florida . . . and if you live in Kentucky, you're likely to end up in Santa!

Use a road atlas to locate these unusual U.S. towns. Determine the nearest large city to each and look up the zip code of the large city in the zip code directory. Record the state abbreviation, nearest large city, and zip codes below.

	State abbrev.	Nearest Large City	Zip code
CHRISTMAS, FLORIDA			
SANTA CLAUS, INDIANA			
GOODNIGHT, TEXAS			
STANDING GROUND, KENTUCKY			
DIFFICULT, TENNESSEE			
CUCKOO, VIRGINIA			
PLUTO, WEST VIRGINIA			
SLAP OUT, ILLINOIS			
BIG CHIEF, CALIFORNIA			
FULLTIGHT, ALABAMA			
BEAVER, LOUISIANA			
WOODSTOCK, VERMONT			
SLIPPERY ROCK, PENNSYLVANIA			
WHYNOT, MISSISSIPPI			

• See page 240 for answers.

240